Rob Roy
MacGregor

Rob Roy MacGregor

Nigel Tranter

Neil Wilson Publishing ● Glasgow ● Scotland

Neil Wilson Publishing Ltd
303 The Pentagon Centre
36 Washington Street
GLASGOW
G3 8AZ

Tel: 0141-221-1117
Fax: 0141-221-5363
E-mail: info@nwp.co.uk
www.nwp.co.uk

A catalogue record for this book is available from the
British Library.

ISBN 1-897784-31-7
Printed in Malta by Interprint

CONTENTS

FOREWORD

The writer on Rob Roy MacGregor is faced with a surprising problem — surprising in that while his subject is famous, known the world over, comparatively little authentic source material is available. Even now not much factual history actually devoted to him has been written, although references to him in works dealing with the contemporary historical scene are legion. The majority of Rob's exploits have been handed down in local tradition, by word of mouth, in the true Gaelic and Highland practice, via what is sometimes called the 'national memory' — by no means the most accurate of media, however excellent a picture it is apt to give of the character of the subject. Sir Walter Scott's renowned novel, with its notes, which has been so largely responsible for spreading the fame of Rob Roy beyond Scotland, is more valuable for its introduction than for the novel itself, which deals with only a small fraction of a long and exciting life — and even so relies heavily on tales collected in the MacGregor country almost a century after Rob's death. To some extent, Scotland's Rob Roy has a resemblance to England's Robin Hood in more than his character and exploits, although the latter may be a wholly legendary figure.

While the main outline of Rob's career is

known and recorded, the author has to pick and choose for his details amongst the great mass of semi-legendary tales, seeking to select what can best be substantiated, what the known events of the times make to seem most likely and what best agrees with his interpretation of the hero's character; an operation allowing scope for considerable latitude in presentation. The following account must be accepted therefore as one man's selection to interpret a complex and somewhat mysterious character.

ONE OF ROB ROY'S SIGNATURES

CHAPTER 1

First Blood — and None Spilt

THE scarlet and orange of a stormy sunset, flaming above the purple-black peaks of Ben Lomond and its attendant mountains, made the young man's fiery red hair positively seem to blaze above his ruddy features. His eyes flashed too, but that was but little the effect of the sunset, for those notably light blue eyes were apt to flash, especially when their owner was roused — which was often. He was roused now, as he pointed back towards a dark knoll behind him, and ordered his score of fierce MacGregor clansmen to retire to its cover — and to keep their steel sheathed. Quietly as he spoke, and in the soft Gaelic, his voice quivered a little, an extraordinarily gentle, even mild voice for so fierce-seeming a character.

His men — or more properly his elder brother's men — did not accept any such unpopular command without question. Highland clansmen did not necessarily obey orders like enlisted soldiers, since each considered himself to be a gentleman and in some sort of kinship to his chieftain. The order to retire, and before a mere rabble of Lowland cottagers, was not such as Highlanders could readily swallow, MacGregors especially, even though the odds might be five to one. A low rumbling growl supported the protest of a giant of a man in ragged tartan and sleeveless calfskin jerkin.

The red-headed young man frowned, and stabbed again with his finger towards the dark, tree-clad hillock, briefly insisting — and though he did not raise his soft voice, there was no mistaking the tenseness or the determination behind it. Then he smiled suddenly, widely, infectiously, and pointed out to his friend Ewan Mor MacGregor that this was a special occasion, that they were here on business after all, and not pleasure.

The tension ebbed at once; the men shrugged, dropped their hands from sword and dirk, some even grinned. Silently, swiftly, like shadows, they slipped away from the last squat, low-browed, thatched cottages of the village of Buchlyvie towards the small birch-grown hummock that lay 100 yards or so northwards, nearer to the vast watery wastes of the Flanders Moss.

Even so, their withdrawal must have been observed, probably by women from some of the nearer cot-houses, for there were high-pitched shouts and an answering roar from the dense throng of men advancing up the narrow village street — the dark moving mass that, in the fading half-light of the sunset, had at first been mistaken for the great herd of cattle for which the MacGregors had been waiting.

Reassembled among the birch trees on the knoll, the fierce group around the young man waited again, the red and green MacGregor tartan of their kilts and plaids hardly distinguishable against the russet bracken and September leafage in the sunset glow. Nevertheless, their presence there was quickly discerned, and the angry, noisy crowd came on towards them, brandishing pitchforks, sickles and cudgels. There might have been 100 villagers against the score of Highlanders.

With exclamations at the insolence of these Lowland clodhoppers, the clansmen were beginning to edge forward again, when once more they were stopped. Despite his commanding ways, the man who restrained them was quite the youngest among them, a mere 20 years old. But for all his open boyish features and silky, carroty beard, he presented no undeveloped or unimpressive appearance. Dressed not in a kilt but in close-fitting trews — long tartan tights that hugged his muscular legs almost as far as the ankle — silver-buckled brogues, a piebald calfskin doublet, MacGregor plaid about chest and one shoulder, and on his head a blue bonnet enhanced by a single up-thrusting eagle's feather, at first sight he seemed to be only of medium height. But a second glance would reveal that he was taller than almost everyone around him — only his height was dwarfed by the enormous width of his shoulders. Unkind critics said that he was in fact deformed, so wide and massive was his torso, so barrel-like his chest above comparatively slender hips and very slightly bowed legs. His was a peculiar physique, certainly, but one that gave a tremendous impression of strength and vigour, an almost sinister quality of aggressive energy that was further reinforced by the extraordinary length of his arms — arms so long that he could tie the garters of his tartan hose without stooping. Armed now with a broadsword hanging on a shoulder-belt, a great dirk at his waist, and a sgiandhu — or lesser dagger — tucked into his garter, his aspect but little matched the gentle lilting voice, and the pleasant friendly smile which transformed his features.

He managed to still his companions' grumbling complaint about the utter unsuitability of running away from a few Lowland peasants by demanding whether any of them had ever seen Rob Roy MacGregor running away from anything — except perhaps Ewan Mor's terrible wife, and even then not so fast as her own husband. And while he still had them smiling he went on more seriously to point out that their chieftain's, his own father's freedom, perhaps even his life, depended on this enterprise. For Glengyle's sake, there must be no mistake this night, no losing of the cattle through any foolish entanglement with the villagers.

It was the year 1691, and Colonel Donald MacGregor of Glengyle, Rob Roy's father, had been a prisoner in Edinburgh Castle for two long years. The Clan Gregor had always been loyal supporters of the royal house of Stewart — Jacobites as they were being called now that King James was an exile in France and 'Dutch William' sat on the throne in London — and Colonel Donald had led a Gregorach regiment in the campaign which collapsed after the Battle of Killicrankie. He had been captured. The Government were now prepared to free him, as they had done most others, for he was an elderly man and ill — but they demanded a large ransom — not all of which would find its way into the Treasury, for government in 1691 was corrupt indeed.

Money, however, was a commodity in which the Glengyle branch of Clan Gregor was somewhat lacking. But if there was one commodity that could most conveniently and profitably be turned into money in the Scotland of that time, it was cattle. The MacGregors were experts on cattle. And a great herd of cattle was due to come along that road at any moment!

All the previous night Rob Roy and his heavily-armed men had hurried secretly from their own mountains of Glengyle and Balquhidder around the head of Loch Lomond, down through the foothill country to the great wide levels of the River Forth, and across the huge wildfowl-haunted marshes of the Flanders Moss. All day they had lain in hiding on the outskirts of this village of Buchlyvie, at a vital point in the drove road which led from Drymen and the West, skirting the great Moss, to Stirling and the East. The Earl of Linlithgow, no friend of the Jacobites, as the MacGregors had learned, had purchased almost the entire entry of beef cattle at the Balloch Fair the day before, and his drovers were driving the beasts back to his east-country estates, almost certainly along this road — over 200 prime steers. Lord Linlithgow had been foolish enough to refuse to continue with his payments of mail, or protection money, to the Glengyle Highland Watch — which was the Gregorach under another name, and a semi-official body which guaranteed the safety of all its clients' cattle, at a price. The highest in the land were more or less prepared to pay this mail since they could by no means protect their herds from Highland cattle-thieves, and the MacGregors could. Lord Linlithgow, then, had to be taught a lesson. Rob Roy's eldest brother John, Younger of Glengyle, was Captain of the Highland Watch.

The cattle should have been past this stage of their journey hours ago, before the Buchlyvie villagers returned home from their work in the fields. Something had delayed the drovers. Unfortunately, a cottar girl had stumbled on a couple of the Gregorach lying in hiding whilst she was herding geese and had given the alarm. Now, the villagers, returning with nightfall, had assembled in wrath. No doubt they believed the lurking intruders to be just a few broken men, stragglers of the defeated Jacobite army, vagabonds, out to filch what they might. Since the failure of the 1689 Rising for the exiled King James, Scotland had been full of broken men, and settled folk everywhere were on their guard against their depredations. These men of Buchlyvie would never have sallied forth thus boldly if they had realised that the strangers were of the feared and terrible Gregorach. But it was most important, from Rob Roy's point of view, that they should not learn it now. For these were Graham folk, the Earl of Montrose's tenants, and Montrose was great with the Government. Everything depended on anonymity.

As the villagers neared the birch knoll, their pace slowed down even as their shouting and fist-shaking grew fiercer. It was one thing to gather and brandish weapons for the defence of hearth and home; but quite another, without discipline or leadership, to undertake a concerted assault on the silent shadowy figures among the dark trees. Few had ambition to be other than the hindmost in such an attack.

Rob listened to the hullabaloo, frowning, tapping a brogued toe on the trampled bracken. He was not yet actually regretting this venture of his — but beginning to wonder whether he might perhaps have been a little hasty. For it was very much all his own responsibility. This was a highly unofficial foray. His brother did not know of it, and undoubtedly would not have approved — even though Lord Linlithgow was so obviously in need of being reminded of the usefulness of the Watch.

A weak Government had set up these Highland Watches — or rather, permitted them to grow — of which the Glengyle one was the most active and successful. They were irregular forces, backed by the authorities in war-torn Scotland after the recent troubles, intended to keep the peace, King William's or anyone else's, in their given areas, by the strength of their own arms. They were especially to put down, if possible, the serious plague of cattle-stealing, which was menacing the reeling economy of the country, by being stronger than the unofficial thieves. On payment, of course, of mail by their protected neighbours. In this area, along the edge of the Highland Line, the fiery MacGregors, hopeless Jacobites as they were, had been the obvious nominees for the task — since they were the most warlike and united, and themselves the most expert cattle-thieves in the land.

But tonight's enterprise was Rob's own idea — indeed it was his first truly independent exploit on a major scale, experienced as he was in the everyday lieutenancy of the Watch. His heart ached for his warrior father, cooped up in a cell in Edinburgh — a living death for any outdoor Highland man. Word of the great sum demanded for his release had spurred his youngest son to this escapade, even if it had not so spurred his eldest son and heir.

It was his own over-eager fighting men who worried Rob now, rather than any threat posed by that rabble. Somehow he must prevent them coming to blows — for once their swords were out there would be no holding his fierce clansmen. It was not that he was frightened of a little blood-letting, in a Scotland where blood had long flowed as readily as water; but so long as his father remained hostage in government hands, the Gregorach must be careful indeed whose blood they shed, especially where the Earl of Montrose was concerned.

Rob decided to try what sweet reasonableness might achieve. 'Wait you now,' he ordered, hand out to hold back his men's almost imperceptible edging forward. 'Not a word out of you. I will speak.' He stepped out a little way, but not sufficiently for him to be beyond the deep shadow of the trees. He raised hand and voice. The gabble and shouting did not diminish.

Rob Roy's normal tones were soft, certainly — but he could bellow like any Gregorach bull out of that great chest when occasion demanded. His roar now shattered the evening. Raggedly the crowd's clamour almost died away.

'Friends,' he called out in English, deep-voiced, now. 'What mean you by this? We offer you no hurt. We have touched nothing of yours.' This was not entirely factual, perhaps, for a duck or two, a few eggs and the like, were folded away in convenient Gregorach plaids as reasonable precaution against night-time hunger on the long road home; but compared with what the MacGregors might have done, this was indeed not worth mentioning. 'We are quiet men, and peaceably disposed.' As well that none of his warriors could speak the English.

A chatter rose from the village throng, and went on rising, with nothing of sympathy or friendliness to it.

Rob Roy's chin rose a degree or two. He was, he believed, a notably reasonable young man, and prepared to put up with a certain amount in the cause of peace and understanding. But to hear himself shouted at as a stot, a gangrel heathen, and worst of all a black Irishman, was too much. It was his educated speech that was largely responsible, probably — for Rob was highly educated for his day, speaking good Latin and Greek as well as English, and with a great fondness for Latin tags. No doubt these yokels, hearing the unexpectedly scholarly English, so unlike their own uncouth version of the language, judged the speaker to be one of King James's disbanded Irish-Catholic mercenaries, a plague to all decent Presbyterian Scots.

'Watch your words, fools!' he rapped out, therefore. 'We are better Scots than your wretched selves — and better men, whatever! So watch you! Back to your holes, vermin!' That was much more honest MacGregor-like talk.

A snarling growl rose from the crowd. A couple of stones came flying through the air, one to hit a birch trunk close to Rob's head.

'As Royal's my Race!' he swore, his own hand dropping to his sword-hilt. As, like a wave of the sea, his clansmen surged up at his back, dark eyes glittering, steel screaming from scabbards and sheaths, Rob made the major effort of his career to date, to take hold upon himself as well as these others, commanding them in Glengyle's name not to move another inch, to leave it to himself.

For seconds the issue hung in the balance. Although a command in their chieftain's name was law to the clansmen, the present group of fighters did not consist of the most amenable of the MacGregors, volunteers for this private enterprise, deliberately chosen for other qualities. Moreover, Rob was very young, little more than a laddie to these veterans of the wars. In that brief but vital moment of decision, another dark figure moved. Up to the youthful leader's side a spare, stooping, lanky man stepped, whose head hung forward in a curious sideways fashion. He put himself at Rob's wide shoulder and turned to face his fellows, silently. No word was spoken.

For the moment the situation was saved. Macanleister, Son of the Arrow-maker, Rob's personal running gillie and henchman, was the sourest, bitterest, most wordless man in Clan Dougal Ciar, the Glengyle branch of Clan Gregor — besides being the most nimble man with a dirk and the best shot with a pistol. He had been Glengyle's own gillie in the wars, and had been wounded when his chieftain was captured. Only with difficulty had he been prevented from voluntarily following his master to prison in Edinburgh. Thereafter he had transferred his peculiar silent allegiance not to the elder and second sons, but to the young Robert Ruadh, Rob Roy. Not always the most gracious or docile of attendants, he sometimes could be worth any dozen other men.

As the Gregorach's inching forward halted and their mutterings sank, Rob turned back to the distant mob, shouting to them that if any of them had any special point to make, any specific complaint, let them come forward and make it to himself.

As he had anticipated, this invitation produced no forward rush — but it did herald another ragged shower of stones. Somebody behind Rob emitted an involuntary gasp of pain. The young man bit his lip. Another one or two such insulting pin-pricks, and there would be no restraining his men, despite Macanleister's support. On an impulse he drew his broadsword right out of its scabbard, tossed it up, caught it expertly one-third way along the blade at the point of balance, and in one swift movement launched it out towards the mob in a fierce explosive throw. There was enormous power in those long arms, and the weapon sailed in a flat arc, whistling through the air, flashing steel catching the last smoky orange-red rays of the sunset in a bloodstained gleam, to curve down and pitch into the earth fully 30 yards away, more than halfway to the seething throng, there to stand erect, quivering, in manifest challenge.

There followed a period of almost complete silence, save for the wind in the trees and the little sigh of approval from sundry MacGregor lips. The light was poor now, but even so the watchers on the knoll could see the front of the villagers' line bend back, away from that symbol swaying above the grass before them.

The silence was quickly broken by a confused gabble — but not before Rob's keen ears had heard something else. His head jerked up — as did others behind him. On the west wind there had drifted the unmistakable sound of the lowing of cattle.

In an instant he was a different man. Gone was indecision and anxiety. He swung round. 'The drove!' he jerked. 'At last! Praise be! Ewan Mor — off with you. All go, but Macanleister. Aye, and Duncan. Behind the houses. To the far end of the village. Take the herd as it enters the narrows of the street. The drovers will be weary, easy game. Hurt as little as you may. Get the beasts running. Hard running. But three of you, four, to get ahead of them. In front. Down the street. Run to this end. You understand? Be waiting for the beasts. Tear thatching off the roofs. Dry thatch. Fired, as the cattle reach these last houses. To turn them this way. You have it? Fire. Smoke. And, mind — no shouting of slogans!'

They replied that they understood.

It must be timed to the moment, he pointed out. They must not light the burning thatch and throw it into the road too soon, or it might turn the herd back. And it must be thrown down only on the far side of the road, just as the first cattle came surging out of the narrows of the street, so as to swing them off the road, free of the houses, northwards in this direction.

No more explicit orders were necessary for these expert cattle-handlers. Like swift ghosts the MacGregors faded away into the gloom of the trees and bushes, leaving only their three companions standing there under the birches. Rob cleared his throat. It now fell to him to do some major talking.

Seeking to mix judicious moderation and firm authority in both words and tone, the young man raised his voice towards the restive and uncertain crowd. He talked as he had never talked before, in a flood of words. He repeated that they were peaceable men, loyal servants of the King — which King he left unspecified. That they wished no hurt to the honest folk of Buchlyvie. That they were here on business, important business, with my Lord Earl of Linlithgow, a great nobleman. That when that business was over they would leave Buchlyvie as though they had never been. They were no Papist Irishry. Heaven forbid! Nor broken men, landlopers, or beggars of any sort. And so on, at much length.

As the spate of speech continued, the crowd began to stir, to murmur again, to lose its fear of that single eloquent sword. Rob had to raise his voice higher, shout louder. When the villagers began, almost imperceptibly at first, to edge forward once more, a shade desperately he cried to them to halt, declaring that if they were determined on a trial of strength then they must choose any two of their number and he would fight them alone, his sword against any weapons they chose.

As he had calculated, this gave them pause for

a little longer, while unwilling champions disclaimed any desire for such fame. Finally, however, they united to howl down the challenge, and stones began to fly again. Rob was nearing his wits' end for wordy invention when, at long last, his flagging talk and their strengthening courage were both overtaken, lost and swallowed up in a greater and more violent uproar which abruptly burst out to westwards, from the other end of the single village street.

With a sigh of relief Rob Roy relinquished distasteful eloquence and squared great shoulders for action.

Thereafter everything happened at great speed. Shouts, yells and screams rising above the sudden bellowing of hundreds of frightened cattle, had turned all the villagers' faces in that direction, when in turn these were submerged under another and still more frightening torrent of sound — the thunder of hooves. Shaking the air, the very ground, confined and magnified by the narrow channel of the cottage-flanked street, growing louder, more terrible every moment, the noise filled the night — and transfixed the crowd, Men stared, appalled, bewildered, unable to move. The village was a few hundred yards in length, consisting of merely this one street, but it took only a few moments for the frightened cataract to traverse the length of it. Lights suddenly appeared in the lee of the last houses, lights which quickly flared into waving torches, and then into flaming fires which seemed to set the very road ablaze. Clouds of acrid smoke came billowing towards the shocked watchers on the westerly breeze. Men began to cough, eyes streaming.

Then the dark, heaving torrent of stampeding cattle burst out from the confines of the houses, eyes gleaming red in the firelight, hooves pounding, horns clashing, nostrils steaming, a cloud of dust rising above. On and on they came, driven by the yelling Gregorach, fanning out into the open ground. But the burning thatch hastily torn from roofs and tossed in their path turned most of them off the road, north by east. Straight for the horror-struck crowd of villagers they surged, terrified, and terrifying. For seconds the men stood as though rooted there. Then, casting away forks and scythes, they turned as of one accord, and ran, every man for himself, tripping and stumbling in the shadows, scattering wide.

Rob Roy and the man Duncan shouted their great laughter. Macanleister never laughed. Rob actually darted forward, through the fleeing throng, towards the oncoming cattle. But only to retrieve his fine broadsword. Then he too, necessarily, turned and ran.

Unlike the others, however, the three Gregorach did not run far. Beyond the birch knoll was a reedy, boggy hollow and then slowly rising land. Plunging across the soft ground they went only a little way further up, to turn and wait, spread out now and pulling off the plaids from their shoulders. They allowed the rise of the knoll to slow up somewhat the trampling steers, the trees to break the solid phalanx of them, and then the soft marshy hollow further to scatter and damp down their impetus. Then, shouting and waving their plaids and darting to and fro, the trio confronted the panting, snorting, floundering brutes as they came lumbering out of the mire. The front rank swerved, hesitated and broke, only a few yards from the yelling Highlanders. Then, bearing to the right, flapping their plaids, the men headed off the bewildered cattle to the left, eastwards. In only a few seconds the mass of beasts was swinging round, plunging back towards the road at a slant. Ewan Mor and the main body of the MacGregors were catching up, roaring with mirth and glee.

In almost less time than it takes to tell, the entire great herd was streaming along the Stirling road towards Kippen, no longer stampeding but at a good heartening trot, under the cloud of their own steam, the Gregorach loping at flanks and rear like so many sheep dogs, grinning their appreciation of it all. Behind there was confusion, wails, smouldering thatches and billowing smoke — but no pursuit.

A bare mile on, a lane turned off which led directly northwards between harvest fields, and then slanted down to end at a deserted mill. Beyond were only the watery wastes of the Flanders Moss, which stretched mile upon mile across the plain of the Forth towards the north and the distant ramparts of the Highland hills. Once into that vast quaking wilderness that only the wildfowl, the roe deer, and the Gregorach knew, where hidden fords, underwater causeways and secret tracks round bogs and meres and lochans guarded the approach to the Highlands, those cattle would be lost to any Lowland ken — until such time as they should re-appear to be sold again at Falkirk Tryst, duly branded with MacGregor markings.

Rob Roy caught up with Ewan Mor as they trotted down into the dark mist-shrouded levels. 'The drovers?' he panted. 'You had no trouble, Ewan?'

'Och, devil the bit, at all,' the big fellow chuckled. 'A few skelps with the flat of our swords, a few sore heads tomorrow, one snapping dog skewered

— that was all of it. Not a drop of blood shed, at all, at all!'

'Good!' Rob nodded. 'Myself, I have a sore throat with much talking!'

CHAPTER 2

Sheep Robbie and Cattle Robbie

SUCCESS, they say, is its own justification — a cynical dictum that was certainly most true in the misgoverned and war-torn Scotland of 1691. Young Rob Roy MacGregor's first and highly individual demonstration of leadership and cattle-thievery in a big way, came to be accepted more or less as a model and exemplar for all time to come. It went down in history as the Herriship (or harrying) of Kippen, in which parish Buchlyvie lies, and was a success by almost any standard save perhaps that of the vexed and difficult question of ethics. Fortunately, that night after the cattle-lifting at Buchlyvie, a brief and accidental encounter with a small picket of suspicious dragoons returning to Cardross at the far side of the Moss, had resulted in nothing more than a headache to add to Rob's sore throat — although, had he not habitually worn a steel plate within his bonnet be would likely have been cut down to the very shoulders by a heavy cavalry sabre, the wielder of which was promptly shot by Macanleister, thus rather spoiling the bloodless record of an otherwise admirably conducted enterprise. But since this disappointing incident took place in fairly thick darkness, the cattle-herders were not identifiable as MacGregors, and no harm was done; the fact that the six remaining troopers bolted post-haste at the fall of their impetuous colleague, probably helped to ensure that no major enquiries were instituted thereafter into the wounding of the corporal in charge. At any rate, the MacGregors heard no more of it.

The cattle all arrived safely and in good order at Glen Gyle, remote amongst its inaccessible mountains between Loch Katrine and Loch Lomond, and proved to be a credit to the Lord Linlithgow's judgment: fine, well-conditioned beasts that in due course would fetch maximum prices at Falkirk sales, 225 of them, with not a really poor one in the lot. Fed and fattened for three weeks on MacGregor oats, some shaggy coats clipped, some heads dehorned, and all branded with the authentic Glengyle mark, they produced not only sufficient to pay the Government's iniquitous charges for entertaining the Laird of Glengyle for two years, but something over — and moreover no single inquiry into their legal ownership, whatever doubts may have been harboured by the chronically suspicious. The Earl of Linlithgow's protests to the Secretary of State produced only polite commiserations and regrets; after all, if the noble Lord could not look after his own livestock, His Majesty's Government could hardly be expected to take on the task.

Cattle-stealing — although of course it was seldom called that, the term 'lifting' or 'reiving' being preferred by all but the late owners — was a major preoccupation in 17th-century Scotland, as indeed it had been for time out of mind. To appropriate someone else's cows was altogether a different matter from, for instance, filching his watch or his money. It was accepted as coming approximately under a category similar to wife-stealing — a personal issue between gentlemen, where final judgments were best deferred. It was an activity, like the other, about which songs, ballads and poems had always been made. Cattle were the sort of commodity that feeble folk who could not hold should not own. The entire clan system of the Highlands was based on the rearing of cattle on the hills, sheep being a very minor consideration, and each clan almost as a matter of duty took its neighbours' cattle when it could. Highlanders looked on Lowlanders' beasts as fairer game still; and Lowlanders, especially Borderers, seldom missed a moonlit night to raid the farms of Northumberland and Cumberland — or the next dale over the hill if time was short.

When the Lord Justice-Clerk of Scotland, Lord Aberuchill, head of the Scottish judiciary and a Campbell to boot, was prepared to pay regular blackmail, as it was called, to the Glengyle Highland Watch to protect his herds, no serious opprobrium could be attached to young Rob Roy MacGregor's name for his methods of raising a wronged father's ransom — especially when he had achieved it with such flair.

History does not record his elder brother's reaction. No doubt John MacGregor, Younger of Glengyle, read Rob a lecture on the dangers of too precipitate private enterprise, where failure might have meant disaster for more than the headstrong adventurer and possible disbandment of the Watch. But, in the circumstances, that would be as far as it could go especially as Rob's reputation and popularity with the clan soared as a consequence.

On the 1st of October 1691 the Privy Council of Scotland gave orders for the release of Lieutenant-Colonel Donald MacGregor, only demanding that he swear first the required oath of allegiance to Dutch King William. Every Highland chief must swear this before New Year's Day anyway, on pain of treason, they insisted. But what was an oath given under duress, and in English, when there was an added rider in good Gaelic, pledging faith instead to the House of Stewart. The Stewarts, that ancient royal house, whose name derived from their former office of High Stewards of Scotland, a name which Mary Queen of Scots had written 'Stuart' merely because she was brought up in France where the letter W did not exist, but which all good Scots continued to spell in proper fashion. Donald MacGregor of Glengyle, the wreck of his former commanding self but still a proud eagle of a man, came home to his own clan and territory at last, amid great rejoicings. And Rob, his youngest son, the apple of his eye, who had made it possible, was the hero of all the glens.

Joy was something of a scarce commodity in the Highlands that winter. The swearing of the oath of allegiance proceeded amongst the glens, and proud chiefs and their clansfolk did not relish the indignity imposed upon them. But instructions from exiled King James advised compliance meantime, and the reprisals after the late fruitless Rising were too recent to be forgotten. Only one chief failed to make his oath in time: old MacIan of the Glencoe MacDonalds, boasting that he would be the last to make it, was held up by snow on his journey to Inveraray, and arrived there three days after the appointed 1st of January 1692. His delayed oath did not appease the Government, although it appeared to do so at the time. A few weeks later 120 soldiers, led by Captain Campbell of Glenlyon, arrived at Glencoe and billeted themselves on the MacDonalds, living with their involuntary hosts for a fortnight in perfectly friendly fashion. Then, one February morning of snow and gale, the blow fell. MacIan was shot dead as he was getting out of bed, his wife immediately thereafter meeting the same fate. Thirty-eight MacDonalds were slain in cold blood that grim morning by their Government guests, from children in arms to old men of 80. Only the darkness and blizzard enabled some to escape to tell the tale. Scotland stood appalled, the Highlands especially. And none more so than the Glengyle MacGregors, who knew well that they were far from beloved of Dutch William's Government — and, worst of all, who could not deny that Campbell of Glenlyon, whose name would be execrated for ever more, even though he acted under superiors' orders, was Glengyle's own brother-in-law, Rob Roy's mother's brother.

Old Glengyle was already an ailing man when he heard the news. MacIan had been an old friend and companion-in-arms of his. Those years cooped up in a cell had been too much for him. He knew that he would not last long now, and desired to demonstrate his affection and gratitude towards his youngest son in some tangible form. But he had little but his lands to leave, and the clan's needs demanded that these pass to his eldest son, the new chieftain. Something had to be done for Rob, however, and his father did the best that he could. A month or two later, to celebrate the young man's 21st birthday, he managed to settle him on a farm of his own.

This holding, unfortunately, could not be in the lairdship of Glen Gyle itself; for though extensive, running to perhaps 25,000 acres, nine-tenths of it was mountain, heather, woodland and bog, and the remaining precarious tenth of possible workable land in such glen-floors as were not covered by water, was already fully taken up by other relations of the chieftain — uncles, brothers, cousins and his two elder sons. Clan Alpine, the parent tribe of the great race of Gregor, once one of the largest and proudest in Scotland, was now largely landless, owing to a chronic failure to select the winning side in innumerable causes, and subsequent persecution by these more shrewd in their allegiances. Land hunger, therefore, was acute amongst the Gregorach, and this branch of the tribe, the Clan Dougal Ciar, the Sons of Brown Dougal, was almost the only group which had managed to cling to its paternal acres — largely, probably, because few envied them their steep barren fastnesses.

There was, however, a large glen lying parallel with Glen Gyle, a few miles northwards over the hills, called Balquhidder. This, after being fought over by various clans, had come into the hands of the Marquis of Atholl, head of the powerful family of Murray. It was occupied by members of many clans, a sort of republic amongst the little clan kingdoms — although there were more MacGregors and MacLarens than most of the others put together. Balquhidder in consequence, was a place of cheerful anarchy, of divided loyalties and considerable lawlessness, from which the Marquis was apt to consider himself lucky to get any rents at all — undoubtedly the least prized of his vast domains. Here the failing Glengyle managed to lease a farm of sorts for young Rob Roy, at a rent which his chronically empty coffers could just afford.

Monachyle Tuarach was perhaps not much of a place even as Highland farms go. Its name means the narrows of the mount, facing north, which will tell its own story. There was, and still is, a small single-storey house with a garret in the roof, a square of steading containing byre, stable and barns, and some hundred steep grassy acres on the south side of the glen, which the sun is not apt to reach much after midday for most of the year. With the water-meadows between Lochs Doine and Voil filling all the valley floor, there was practically no arable land to grow winter feed for cattle — a circumstance which undoubtedly was largely responsible for the farm being vacant in the first place. It would not be every pastoralist's idea of an earthly paradise.

Rob Roy, however, was well content. Of an independent frame of mind, he wanted to be on his own — for various reasons. Monachyle was only eight miles from Glen Gyle, with a handy little pass through the hills which he could traverse on a garron, a sure-footed Highland pony, in an hour. So he could continue to engage in clan activities and play his part in the Watch.

It was, indeed, largely what Rob had learned in the Watch that made him well enough pleased with his new farm. Rob had a nimble mind for more than banditry and Latin tags — moreover, he was of an impatient temperament. Observing, considering, and putting two and two together, he had perhaps not unnaturally come to the conclusion that the slow, painstaking business of growing crops and breeding cattle was not for such as himself. Cattle dealing was the thing — trading, buying and selling, droving. That was where profits were to be made — especially for a MacGregor, who could be reasonably sure that his own and his clients' cattle would not suffer interference, at home or on the road. Moreover, if other beasts, less conventionally acquired, came his way, they would be the more conveniently dealt with by an established dealer. Monachyle, with its upland pastures and water-meadows, would serve adequately as a base, to assemble and feed up his purchases, to rest his droves, to provide a safe headquarters for a man of initiative — for no constables, sheriff-officers or other minions of authority, less than a full squadron of cavalry, would dare to penetrate so far into unruly Balquhidder.

At the May term, then, of 1692, Rob Roy, Macanleister and one or two carefully selected choice spirits, settled in at the little farmery under the hill. Neighbours, even Balquhidder neighbours, tended to look thoughtful, and counted their livestock with more than usual care. Without capital, of course, Rob had to start business in a modest way. It was sensible, also, to restrict himself to fairly orthodox trading at first. Sheep were cheaper to buy and sell than cattle; therefore, as far as dealing went, he tended to concentrate on sheep to begin with. The red-headed, pleasant-faced if curiously-built young Highland man, with his tough-looking companions, became a well-known figure at sheep sales and markets from Inverness to Glasgow, and as far south as Galloway and the Borderland. None found occasion to distrust him; his word was his bond; he never claimed that clients' beasts had died on the way — a favourite assertion of drovers; he delivered the goods; and none lost their stock while it was in Sheep Robbie's care.

This was a nickname dubbed on him by some Lowland wit — although it was not one which many men would dare use to the bearer's face.

Rob, like most other Highlanders, was punctilious about modes of address. He gave others their proper designation, and expected the same courtesy for himself. If men could not call him Mr MacGregor, they could say Robert Ruadh or Rob Roy; but MacGregor itself, alone and unadorned, was not admissible since it implied the chiefship of all the MacGregors; and anything like Sheep Robbie was not to be endured for a moment.

Highland susceptibilities and pride are matters which Lowland Scots and Englishmen still have to take into consideration. Few Highlanders fail to consider themselves gentlemen, whatever their financial background, the ownership of mere money being but little esteemed north of the Highland line. Rob, as son of a chieftain of a sept or branch clan, expected a decent respect.

He had his own way of emphasising this. That the offender might hold high position did not affect the issue. For example, it is told how even his own landlord was not immune from education in this matter. The Marquis of Atholl was old, and his great estates were now under the management of his eldest son, the Lord Murray — who, as it happened, was also Secretary of State for Scotland, the Government's principal representative. Despite all this, however, Murray was unwise enough not only to refuse to pay protection money to the Glengyle Highland Watch — which, after all, the Government had set up — but to make disparaging remarks about MacGregor honesty. One night, a flock of 350 prime sheep disappeared without trace from Atholl property in upper Glen Almond, near Crieff — and nobody would hazard a guess as to where they might have gone.

Not until next market-day at Crieff, that is. Lord Murray was there in person, and complained bitterly of his loss to John Menzies of Shian, one of Atholl's largest tenants.

Perhaps Shian had had a drink or two, after a successful sale, for he was imprudent enough to comment in a voice loud enough to be heard by others, at the market-cross of Crieff. 'Och, my lord — you have but yourself to blame, I'm thinking,' he said. 'Our friend Sheep Robbie would likely ken the whereabouts of your wethers — if indeed he had not his own hand at them, whatever!'

Menzies of Shian was not long in ruing that remark. Rob's intelligence system was very good, and he heard of it all quickly.

'Sheep Robbie, am I, to Shian?' he cried, when informed of it. 'As Royal's my Race, it will be Cattle Robbie he'll be calling me next!'

And that very night, Shian's entire herd of cattle vanished from their pastures in Glen Quaich, 10 miles north of Crieff. No-one ever traced the thieves or the beasts — although there was no lack of people to venture an opinion. But they tended to do it in a whisper.

Rob Roy was beginning to develop his own moral code, nevertheless, however peculiar. He had a soft heart for those in adversity, in need, or suffering under persecution. His was an essentially practical mind, and his sympathy took practical form. What are nowadays called the under-privileged, in the area in which he operated — old people, the infirm, widows and orphans and the like — began to bless his name. Flanks of mutton, haunches of venison or beef, or a bag of meal, in hard times or at New Year, usually delivered anonymously at night; a couple of lambs to replace casualties in a tiny flock; a new cow when the old one had gone dry — these were the sort of gestures which Rob Roy liked to make towards the unfortunate. Some may say that perhaps it was done to soothe his conscience; but the probability is that, as far as cattle-lifting and the like was concerned, his conscience troubled him not one whit.

Busy as he was with his farming and dealing and droving, his lieutenancy of the Watch and his clan activities, Rob still found time for one other preoccupation — courting. He had long had an admiration for the other sex, and especially for a dark-eyed and dark-haired far-out cousin of his own, Mary MacGregor of Comar. Now, with an establishment of his own to run, and a growing business bringing him financial independence, like other young men before and after, he recognised the need for a wife rather than mere pleasant dalliance. Macanleister and his other assistants were all very well, on the road or the hill; but of a long winter evening, something more cosy was called for.

There has been much nonsense talked and written about Rob Roy's romance. Strangely enough, this is mainly the great Sir Walter Scott's fault. He was one of the finest storytellers of all time, and a man who did an enormous amount for both Scotland and the novel. But on the subject of Rob Roy MacGregor, he was by no means at his best. Which is a pity, for, because of his prestige, much that he wrote has been taken almost for gospel, and much that he missed out has been hardly accepted as ever having happened. To a very large number of people his novel and play of Rob Roy are all that they know of 'the Highland freebooter', as Scott dubbed our hero — who was in fact so very much more than any freebooter. The novel deals only with a very brief period of Rob's long and exciting career — and not by any means the most important part of it. Admittedly the notes to the novel do more justice to the man, and cover a longer period, but they are superficial in presentation — and how many people read them? The play made out of the novel is still better known, and here no notes really apply. The film and television interpretations of Rob Roy's career, until the latest motion picture from United Artists, have all been based on Scott, and therefore only perpetuate and underline the inadequacy of it all. It is like interpreting Napoleon by recounting only his behaviour in one battle.

Scott's picture of Rob's wife is far from flattering — and he doesn't even get her name right. He calls her Helen, whereas her true name was Mary. How he came to make this mistake about the name is not to be known — but the register of Buchanan parish, where the marriage banns were proclaimed, gives the true name of Mary, spelt in the form of Marie as often done in Scotland.

Scott made his Helen a woman of fierce and violent character. It is very doubtful if this was so. Strong in character almost certainly she was — no unusual attribute in Highland women. And her later sufferings were terrible enough to have permanently soured her temper. But though they may have done so for a while, they did not do so permanently. Despite this period in middle life when she seems to have been at odds with her rather overpowering husband, in the main she was a most faithful and loving wife, patient to a high degree. Rob remained devoted to her to the day of his death. He cannot always have been the easiest of husbands, either.

MacGregor of Comar, Mary's father, was a second cousin of Glengyle's, and occupied a remote and wild property tucked away under the east flank of Ben Lomond itself, 15 miles south of

Balquhidder, inaccessible then as it is today —
surely a most inconvenient place for courting,
however suitably solitary. However, Mary seems
to have spent much of her time at her uncle's farm
of Corryheichen on the shores of Loch Arklet,
much nearer to Glen Gyle and a reasonable place
to reach. Probably she realised all too clearly that
no young men were likely to find their way very
frequently to Comar. The little grey cottage under
the hill, at the lochside, is still pointed out as the
house from which Rob Roy carried off 'Helen'
MacGregor; but it is not in the least likely that he
had to do any carrying-off. They were married
perfectly normally and respectably at Corryarklet,
the township across the loch where another brother of her father was laird, at New Year 1693.

Monachyle Tuarach in Balquhidder now had a
mistress, and no doubt became a more respectable
place in consequence.

Soon after this, old Glengyle died. This had a
great effect on Rob. Not only did he lose his
admired and beloved father, but his whole life
changed notably. His brother John now became
chieftain of the Clan Dougal Ciar, and had neither
the time nor the inclination to continue as Captain
of the Glengyle Highland Watch. It is not known
what became of the second son, Duncan; perhaps
he was not strong, or not adventurously inclined.
At any rate, he drops out of history. Rob Roy
moved tip to take over the Watch.

Now he was in a position to make his presence
felt on quite a wide swathe of Scotland.

CHAPTER 3

Capture — and Escape

FOR the next few years, Rob was a busy man. Scotland smouldered, always about to burst into flame but never quite doing so. All the time, revolt and civil war were just below the surface. The Government in London was feeble; it was savage, fluctuating, riddled with jealousies and suspicions, personal animosities and divided loyalties. Ever since 1603, on the death of the childless Queen Elizabeth, when King James VI of Scotland, Mary Queen of Scots' son, had succeeded his faraway cousin to the English throne and so became James I of the United Kingdom, Scotland had been more and more neglected as to government. Moving down to London, the Stewart Court had taken much of its power and influence with it, and though the Scottish Parliament still existed, it had never been such a powerful body as that of England, and the King's rule predominated. So when the Revolution of 1688 took place in England and Catholic King James II and VII was driven away by the Protestant English Parliament, and the Dutch William of Orange was brought to the throne instead, there was much bitterness in

Scotland — for this foreign king could be expected to misrule and neglect Scotland still further. And he did. There had been continuous murmurings in the northern kingdom ever since his accession, and open revolt in 1689. The aftermath of Killiecrankie had only damped down this unrest.

Now, central authority could be exercised only sketchily in the Lowlands and scarcely at all in the Highlands. Religious differences between Presbyterians, Episcopalians and Catholics rent not only the kingdom but districts, clans and families. Taxes were collected for both King William and King James. Money was scarce and prices high. Men did not know which way to turn — but those who did, had room to manoeuvre to some effect.

Robert Ruadh MacGregor knew which way he wanted to turn. He was a convinced Jacobite and probably a Catholic at heart. But he had seen the price his father had had to pay for his loyalty to the House of Stewart, and saw no point in paying it all over again. He kept his politics, like his religion, under his bonnet, difficult as this was.

He is not altogether to be blamed, perhaps, for this prudent attitude. He had an enemy at the head of the Government in Scotland, Lord Murray, the Secretary of State, his own landlord. Moreover, the Clan Alpine, the entire race of MacGregor, was once more in a highly dangerous situation. The proscription of the name had been reintroduced just a few weeks before Glengyle died.

To understand just what this meant, it is necessary to go back another 100 years or more. As has been indicated, the MacGregors had been on the losing side in most of the struggles for power in Scotland over a long period — through lack of political judgment rather than any lack of valour. Most of their wide lands had been taken by others, notably the great Clan Campbell, which had cornered nine-tenths of them. Much of this had been achieved by shady legal manoeuvres rather than by right of conquest, for the MacGregors had never troubled to invest in legal charters and papers to prove their ownership of their age-old territories, and the Campbells were always expert at manipulating the law. The sheepskin, not the sword was the Campbells favoured weapon — sheepskins being used in the old days for writing charters upon.

To protect their gains, the Campbells prevailed on successive Kings of Scots to grant Letters of Fire and Sword against their victims, in effect outlawing the entire race. This did not mean a great deal so long as the MacGregors stayed in their own Highlands where the Government's writ did not run anyway; but it did mean that the law was always against them, and as the rule of law increased, so Clan Alpine diminished. Then, in James VI's time, matters were brought to a head by a particular piece of MacGregor brigandage which united their many enemies. The entire clan was proscribed. Even the name was forbidden by Act of Parliament. None could legally call themselves MacGregor; all must adopt another surname. None was permitted under pain of death, to carry any weapon, even for self-defence, other than a blunt eating-knife. Anyone who slew a MacGregor could not be punished — indeed Government rewards were paid for MacGregor heads brought in, and bloodhounds were imported to hunt them down. That the Nameless Clan survived at all is something of a miracle, and a tribute to the toughness of the race.

This state of affairs persisted until the Restoration of King Charles II, when the Act of

Proscription was repealed; this was because of the good work done by the MacGregors in aiding Montrose in the royal cause and the Civil War. It was astonishing how loyal they remained to the Stewarts, who had never done anything for them — quite the reverse, indeed. For the next 30 years, men could proudly call themselves MacGregor again; not that they had ever ceased to do so, but legal documents, such as charters of land and so on could now bear the name once more.

In 1693, however, King William's Government abruptly reintroduced the Act, with all its ferocious clauses. Whether it was done on Lord Murray's advice is not known, but it does not seem improbable, for he made no secret of his grudge against the MacGregors, which was of much older standing than merely the loss of his 350 sheep. The old high chief of Clan Alpine had died, and his successor, MacGregor of Kilmanan, had bought the large property of Craigrostan, on the east side of Loch Lomond adjoining Glen Gyle. Possibly the authorities feared that this, together with the growing power of the Glengyle Watch, heralded a strengthening of the clan. Government policy was always to weaken the Highlands, by any and all means, as a breeding ground of support for the exiled Stewarts. So the blow fell, only a few months after the dire Massacre of Glencoe.

No doubt they would have disbanded the Watch too, only the pockets of many members of the Government were involved, cattle being one of the few stable sources of wealth in 17th-century Scotland. Without the Watch's protection, lairds north of the Forth and Clyde could not sleep easy in their beds of a night. Rob, then, had to walk with infinite care, playing one factor against another, skilfully balancing pros and cons. He played not only factors and policies, but men; the highest in the land. Since he could not own or occupy land or sign the merest receipt in the name of MacGregor, he was forced to adopt another surname for business purposes, as were all those of his race of any degree whatever. Most found it convenient to take the name of their landlord or of the dominant house in their district, and the majority of MacGregors in Perthshire called themselves Murray in consequence. Not so Rob Roy. He did not even name himself Graham — the family name of the Marquis of Montrose — as did his brother, although Glen Gyle was in the territory nominally under the sway of that nobleman.

Instead, he chose the name of Campbell, despite its hated sound in MacGregor ears. Admittedly this was his mother's name, but that was not why he selected it. He did so deliberately in order to place himself in some measure under the guardianship of the Earl of Breadalbane, the chief of the mid-Scotland branch of Clan Campbell, and Murray's great rival in the area. It must have astonished many. However, Rob chose his name with considerable shrewdness.

Quickly, the new direction of the Watch made itself felt. What had been casual and haphazard became close-knit and efficient. In the past, the Watch, like others of its kind, had been a sort of irregular police force, with special reference to cattle-stealing and the responsibility to keep under control other forms of thievery and violence in its neighbourhood, the costs of which were met, not by the Government but by the landowners and farmers whose cattle were protected. No large sums were collected in this way, and the Watches were popular with their captains and members not for financial reasons, but because they enabled them legally to go about armed, imposing their will on their neighbours, and keeping their heads high. Also, it provided an excellent training for clansmen who might well be involved in more serious military activities in due course. Without sacrificing this last advantage, Rob changed all this, as far as the Glengyle Watch was concerned.

From now on, the Watch and business were more or less combined. Every landholder and farmer, great and small, in the area — and in time Rob stretched his area as far as it would go — was visited, assessed and given good advice, being left in no doubt that he would be well advised to join the subscribers to the Watch. He was given a careful calculation of the sum he would require to pay annually. There were to be no more vague, optional or intermittent payments. Each was expertly assessed on his acreage, numbers of beasts carried, and ability to pay. This was insurance, a serious business arrangement. Those who paid — and in time they were the vast majority — were assured that their herds would graze safely at all times, travel safely to markets, and be expertly driven; for, of course, he looked after the droving too. If, for one reason or another, any beasts fell by the wayside, they would be compensated. That these compensation animals would come from those who had been foolish enough not to join the scheme was not likely to be proved. The standards of payment were raised — but so were the services rendered.

Those who refused were warned that they were injudicious indeed; they would not be protected and who could tell what robbers and ruffians might sally forth from Highland hideouts to attack their flocks and herds? That such attacks did follow upon refusal to pay, most promptly and regularly, left the unkind whispering that of course Rob organised it himself, and that while Rob as Captain of the Watch guarded men's cattle, Rob as leader of unattached MacGregors ensured that men's cattle indeed needed guarding. Undoubtedly the Watch was never anywhere near when such raids took place — yet the moment chastened owners toed the line, depredations ceased.

It took months and years, of course, to build up this organisation to the pitch of effectiveness which Rob desired. There were, at first, many who had to learn the hard way. But as time went on, pride was apt to be pocketed, and even hardened, proud and obstinate men saw the light. They recognised that, on his own terms, they could trust Rob. He was reliable. He worked what was in effect a great co-operative scheme. In the unsettled state of the country, cattle amounted to wealth, the best investment against almost every contingency. With Rob Roy's aid men could rear and market their cattle almost without fear — which was something new in Scotland. His charges were high but not exorbitant.

Moreover, he kept the neighbourhood free from many other forms of trouble. Over many hundreds of square miles of Central Scotland peace of a sort prevailed — Rob Roy's peace. It was the successful initiation of what in modern times has been called the protection-racket — and few of the 20th-century operators in Chicago or elsewhere worked it out so thoroughly and so fairly as Robert MacGregor Campbell.

Rob prospered and Glen Gyle prospered, although as a whole Scotland's prosperity was ebbing fast. Even the new high chief of Clan Alpine, Kilmanan, prospered, despite the fact that he was a feckless, improvident man and little better than a drunken roisterer. Rob took over the management of Kilmanan's large estate of Craigrostan and Inversnaid as a sort of factor, for the clan's sake. Though this added much to his work, it also added to his power. He was now considerably more influential, within and without the clan, than was his brother Glengyle.

All this was not achieved without jealousy and hostility, of course. Scots being Scots, there were many attempts at independent action, and not a few groupings together to challenge Rob's monopoly. But he held the great advantage of the Watch, almost as good as a private army. His high opinion of himself as a gentleman, however, restricted his use of this to counter those who acted against him; to those who merely spoke against him, he used other tactics where he felt that they ought not to be ignored. When his intelligence system informed him of such — and he did not miss much — it was his habit to seek them out personally and challenge them to put the matter to the test as gentlemen should, with their swords. He had made himself a very expert swordsman — and his enormous length of arm aided him. But, though he is known to have fought more than 20 duels, he was no killer, and is not reported ever to have slain anyone thus — something of a record for that duelling age.

He did not always win, however. One night he met his match, and by mere chance. He enjoyed good fellowship, and on this occasion, dropped in at the inn of Arnprior, near Buchlyvie. Here he met, and took an instant dislike to a young and dandified laird named Harry Cunningham of Boquhan, dressed in the height of Lowland extravagance. When this exquisite gentleman, who had drunk more than he should, began to express

Whig and anti-Jacobite sentiments too loudly, Rob found it necessary to rebuke him before all. Cunningham must have been very brave, or very drunk, for he promptly slapped Rob Roy's face.

A duel could be the only result, and at once. There was a problem here, for it turned out that the laird's sword could not be found — in fact it had been taken away and hidden by the goodwife of the inn, so she presumably knew its owner's habits and wanted to keep her establishment free of trouble. Either no-one was willing to lend him one, or all other bearers of swords quietly betook themselves off, for the only weapon that could be found for him on the premises was an old rapier used for poking the fire. With this, nevertheless, he took on the redoubtable MacGregor.

Cunningham of Boquhan must have been a swordsman indeed, for drunk as he was, and thus armed, he in fact out-fought Rob Roy. Perhaps Rob was even more drunk — although this was not a failing of his. At any rate, he had the worst of it, on this occasion, and was actually slightly wounded in the stomach by the poker-rapier, staggering back against the inn door which collapsed under his weight and landed him his length in the mud outside. It is perhaps illustrative of Rob's character, despite this public discomfiture, that he picked himself up, came back into the hostelry, congratulated the victor and shook hands with him, bought him a drink and remained drinking with him for the rest of the night. Thereafter, these two are reported to have been the best of friends.

It should be mentioned that Rob habitually fought with the Highland broadsword, a heavy weapon probably more apt for real warfare than duelling, and in the confined space of an inn parlour a slender rapier, even one that had seen better days, in a nimble wrist, might well have a great advantage of speed.

That Rob's fame with the broadsword was of no mere local renown is proved by the fact that the great MacNeil of Barra, 38th of his line and chief of his name, proudest of all the island chiefs, left his Hebridean isle and came all the way south to Loch Lomond-side especially to put this fame to the test. Demanding to know where he could find Mac-Gregor, this notable warrior actually ran Rob to earth at the market of Killearn only 16 miles north of Glasgow, and promptly challenged him to a duel with broadswords there and then in the public street.

Rob protested at first that he was busy, and never in any case fought without a cause. But the other would have none of it, declaring that he had come hundreds of miles for this purpose, and demanding to know if the MacGregor was afraid.

That, of course, was that. Without more ado they fell to, no doubt to the great interest and excitement of all at the market. It was a long and fierce struggle, for MacNeil was, needless to say, a brilliant broadsword himself. But in the end it was Rob's sword which won the day, snaking past the older man's vigilant guard and slicing his sword-arm at the elbow. It would be interesting to know how the proud islander took his beating, but all that we are told is that he lay convalescing at Killearn for many weeks, presumably until he could return to Barra without being too obviously wounded and defeated.

This chief, Roderick Dhu, or the Black, was as staunch a Jacobite as was Rob, having been 'out' with Dundee at Killiecrankie, and therefore a com-panion-in-arms of Rob's father. He also played a prominent part in the later Rising of 1715, in which

Rob also took a large share — so that the pair were to see a deal of each other in the future.

Not all men could be dealt with by means of the sword, or even the Watch, however. The biggest challenge and problem of them all, of course, was John, Lord Murray, the Secretary of State. Rob had prudently kept pretty well out of Murray's way for some time, but the other had by no means forgotten him. Murray was only waiting his time to catch Rob out in some situation where his captaincy of the Watch would not save him. In May, 1695 he got his opportunity.

Strangely enough, it is difficult to trace the exact reason or excuse for Murray's action, and why he suddenly decided that he had sufficient evidence against the MacGregor to risk a show-down. Perhaps Rob had been less discreet than usual — if that is a term that may be used about Rob Roy MacGregor. Perhaps there had been treachery. At all events, Murray wrote to his mother that he had the information which he needed, but indicating that official action had to be pursued with considerable care. He recorded:

> *I have sent a party to apprehend that Rob: Campbell, I have not yet heard what they have done. I believe Breadalbin indeed is his friend because he has taken his name, and his lordship has espoused his interest wherefor I wish none of his lordship's friends at Dunkeld may get notice I employed about him.*

The Secretary of State must have thought well and long before this operation, for it was most efficiently planned. Probably wisely — for Rob was a most difficult fish to catch unawares — he decided that his enemy would be most likely to be least on his guard and unsuspecting when at his own home at Monachyle. But Balquhidder was a hard nut to crack. No direct approach up the glen was possible; Rob would be warned and away long before any government party, however strong, could be half-way to his farm. Accordingly, Murray employed a man called Duncan MacEown, who was conversant with all the area, and knew the high passes and secret tracks about the head of Balquhidder, to lead a troop of selected dragoons by devious ways through the mountains — no light task for heavy cavalry horses. But luck was with them in this enterprise. One morning, the troopers slipping down from the misty hillsides, quietly surrounded the farmhouse, and when the officer and MacEown presented themselves at the front door, it was Rob himself, unarmed and unsuspicious, who opened to them.

There does not seem to have been any struggle. No doubt Rob saw that anything of the sort would be as hopeless as it was undignified. Mary would have had to suffer indignity also, undoubtedly, and this was bound to weigh with him. Where Macanleister and the other close Gregorach stalwarts were this misty morning is not reported. At any rate, Rob yielded quietly, was set upon a horse, and surrounded by armed dragoons was led off down the glen, the troopers having orders to shoot him down at the first sign of trouble. Eyes must have opened wide too late in Balquhidder that day, at such a sight.

The MacGregor seemed to be slumped in dejection, as well he might be. The troop turned southwards where Balquhidder glen joins the wider valley of Strathyre — bonnie Strathyre of the song. This was the road to Stirling and Edinburgh. Strathyre is a long glen, its lower half almost wholly filled by the four-miles-long loch of Lubnaig. Then there is the short Pass of Leny, and abruptly the mountains end and it is open rolling country from Callander southwards.

There had been neither time nor opportunity for Rob to get any message out to either the Watch or his clans-people at Glen Gyle to effect any kind of rescue. Although undoubtedly word of the capture would speed swiftly across the little pass to Glen Gyle, long before any body of men large enough to tackle a troop of dragoons could assemble and come in pursuit, the soldiers and their prisoners would be out through the Pass of Leny and into the safe settled Lowland countryside where anything short of a pitched battle must fail to effect a release. Anyway, to bring the Watch into it, in a direct clash with Government forces, whether successful or not, would indubitably be the end of the Watch. Rob was on his own — and looked it, head hanging in depression as he was trotted off to captivity as his father had been before him. Once in Murray's hands in Edinburgh, there was little doubt that, whatever charge they liked to lay against him, it would be long before he smelled the Highland heather again.

Rob may have been downcast at the turn of events, angry with himself for allowing it to happen — but his mind was far from dwelling on his misfortunes. He was in fact going over, before his mind's eye, every foot of the road before it reached the Pass of Leny. It did not take him very long to reach a decision. He continued to look hang-dog in the saddle, however — in fact, he made his horsemanship to appear quite deplorable, jouncing about like a mounted sack of potatoes.

In those days the road down Loch Lubnaigside was a mere slender winding track — but a track which Rob Roy knew like the palm of his own hand. Between his captors he trotted and jolted humbly down almost a couple of miles of the loch's length, so that even if they might have feared trouble initially, they were lulled into belief that their prisoner's spirit was gone. At numerous points they were forced to ride in Indian file. The troopers were not fools, of course; at such places those immediately in front and behind their captive drew and cocked their heavy cavalry pistols.

At length the cavalcade, now inevitably much strung out, drew near a spot where the track rose quite high above the loch, with a long and almost sheer drop below to rocks at the water's edge. Round a little headland here the path was narrow indeed, with loose stones fallen from the bank above, which all but overhung. Those rocks below must have looked thoroughly unpleasant to all concerned especially when the captive's horse began to fancy-dance and fidget temperamentally at the narrowest part, presumably on account of the drop below and the loose stones beneath its hooves. Other horses can be easily affected by such tantrums and the dragoons directly in front and behind, cursing, gave the brute a wide berth. Slouched heavily in the saddle as he was, it looked indeed as though the unhappy rider could barely keep his seat. The rocks below in that case, might well save the Secretary of State an expensive trial.

Rob's hectic clutching at his beast was in reality vicious nipping and scratching at its sweating coat. As the ill-used charger reared and curvetted in alarm, the men in front pushed ahead, lest the wretched brute bolt into them out of control and send them toppling down the cliff; those behind held back for the same reason, seeking to calm steeds rapidly becoming uneasy at what they saw.

Where the bank above hung low over them, in seemingly the very worst position, Rob sprang into life. Sprang in deed and in truth, up off his mount's heaving back. It was extraordinary that any man could, from a sitting position astride a saddle, leap so abruptly upwards — and leap so high. His great length of arms helped, of course, for somehow he grabbed the stout heather that grew there and with another explosive sideways jerk, swung himself bodily up on to the bank, a shower of earth and gravel descending from his hands and knees as they scrabbled for holds and purchase.

Not a single pistol-shot cracked out, then or later. The troop was now a lengthy twisting line. Of those in front, probably only three or four would have been able to see what went on — had they been looking behind them; which they were not, for obvious reasons. Only a few of those behind had rounded the little headland, and of these only the first two might have been able to shoot without endangering their fellows. But these were far too busy controlling their restive mounts and wondering what the prisoner's brute was going to do on that perilous track, to take difficult aim from their lurching saddles. Anyway, their only target was a pair of white, convulsively-kicking kilted legs — a poor mark at the best. Very quickly even these were gone from their sight, over the upward curve of the bank.

The situation was an extremely awkward one for organising swiftly any pursuit. To have been at all effective, the nearest troopers would have needed to be equally agile, desperate, and as good at jumping as was Rob Roy — which, apart from anything else, their long and heavy leather cavalry thigh-boots made impossible. If they had jumped, and missed reaching the bank above, the chances were that it would have been the rocks below for them. At all events, none tried it, shouting their alarm instead and pressing onwards. But shouts round a corner of narrow track are not always intelligible. These had the effect of halting those just in front. Some tried to turn their horses back; others contented themselves with gazing behind from their saddles. The excited oncoming riders inevitably became entangled with their forward colleagues — and there was no room for any sort of entanglement on that path. Confusion reigned, and there was an almost complete standstill. The officer in charge, away in front, could only shout in return and gaze back helplessly — while nobody could tell his sergeant in the rear what was going on round the bend.

Needless to say, none of them clapped eyes on Rob Roy again. The hillside was and still is heavily wooded, and by the time that some kind of search could he instituted by dismounted men, the trees had long since swallowed him up. Anyway, even if they could have spotted him, it is almost unthinkable that they could have caught Rob in his own heather, especially hampered by their heavy boots. In fact, he contoured along the hillside in the cover of the woods, then slipped down to the water-side at the head of the loch, and crossed the shallows hidden by reeds and alders there. Once on the west side, there was nothing between him and Monachyle Tuarach save six or seven miles of birch woods, deer-hair grass and heather, however steeply sloping. He was home in a couple of hours, with Mary sobbing relief in his long arms.

He did not linger long in telling the tale. By the time that the harassed captain of dragoons and his troop had arrived back at the farm, Rob and Mary were gone. Every cattle — beast, sheep and garron was gone — as was the poultry. And a great crowd of hostile Balquhidder men were gathered round the house, growling threats and insults at the military. Circumspectly, however reluctantly, the soldiers took their leave and headed back whence they had come, to face Lord Murray's wrath.

CHAPTER 4

For King James or King William?

IT was, on the face of it, surprising how few were the repercussions to this stirring episode, or at least, the evident repercussions. Apart from the fact that Rob kept Mary away from Monachyle for a while, it was almost as though it had all never happened. No more troopers came to Balquhidder, Glen Gyle or Craigrostan; perhaps Lord Murray did not want to risk advertising one failure with another. In fact, he probably disclaimed all connection with the incident, in the fashion of politicians. It was some time before Rob Roy allowed himself to be seen in populous places like markets and town streets without a sizeable bodyguard of husky MacGregors — but otherwise he continued his activities as before. Indeed the Watch was especially active, notably on the perimeter of the vast Atholl estates, where a sudden and unaccountable outbreak of thievery began to decimate the cattle herds of the old Marquis and his tenants, demanding the Watch's intervention. Soon deputations of tenants were calling upon the old Lord and his son Murray, urging them to become subscribers to the Glengyle Watch, for self-preservation's sake a thing which father and son had resolutely refused to consider hitherto. Rob did not yet risk bringing Mary back to Monachyle, although he resumed use of the place for grazing and droving purposes; but there were plenty of hospitable houses deep in MacGregor territory where they were welcome to stay, especially at Inversnaid, inaccessible on the eastern shore of Loch Lomond and the main house of Kilmanan, the chief's Craigrostan estate, where Rob was now almost as good as master.

So a precarious balance prevailed — though on the surface all was calm and normal. Everyone knew that the Government, egged on by Murray, would clip Rob's wings if it could; and Rob was not the man to forget the attack made upon him on Murray's orders. One day there must be an accounting, one way or the other. When it happened, it could be expected to be dramatic.

Strangely enough, however, there was in fact no accounting nor dramatics — none that have ever been recorded. It is one of the minor mysteries of history how Rob Roy MacGregor, the Highland freebooter, and Lord Murray, soon to be created Earl of Tullibardine and Viscount Glenalmond by a grateful monarch in his father's lifetime, came to terms and buried the hatchet. It seems the unlikeliest thing to have happened; two proud men with a long history of family and personal animosity, one at the pinnacle of his career as ruler of Scotland, the other all but an outlaw, his very name forbidden him, coming together abruptly and agreeing not only to let bygones be bygones, but in fact to co-operate from then onwards.

But that is what happened. Murray, it seems, was the one to open negotiations. He used another

MacGregor who had adopted his own surname of
Murray, as a go-between, and Rob was offered a
complete pardon, a wiping clean of the slate, safe-
conduct, and great advantages in the future — all
so long as he merely made a formal statement of
regret for past disturbances of the King's peace and
acknowledged the authority of the Government.

On the face of it, this seems hardly credible. But
it was true, and there was no catch in it. To prove
this beyond doubt, an official Bond was to be
drawn up, in the usual Highland manner, with
lofty witnesses to its signing, so that it could not be
repudiated by either party. It is interesting to note
that one of these witnesses was the later famous
Simon Fraser, Lord Lovat, one of the most intriguing characters in Scottish history, who was eventually executed in London for his part in the Jacobite
Rising of 1745. Rob's guarantors or sureties were
the no less notable individuals of Alexander
MacDonnell of Glengarry, chief of one of the greatest branches of Clan Donald, and Alexander,
brother of the new MacIan of Glencoe. There is
something significant about these three names, as
we shall hear presently.

There have been criticisms of the seemingly
subservient terms of the wording of the Bond
which Rob Roy duly signed before these witnesses, at Dunkeld House, Murray's home, on June
22nd, 1695. For a proud chieftain it may, today,
seem over-submissive. But it must be remembered
that this was how even the highest in the land did
write in those days, when a victorious general
could sign himself to a defeated enemy as '... I
have the honour to be, with very great respect my
lord, your lordship's most obedient and most
humble servant', and kings and prime ministers
themselves penned such florid sentiments.

The Bond was wordy and lengthy, but it does not make very clear just what advantages Rob was getting out of it all — understandably, perhaps, for it was in effect committing the Government to an attitude that it could hardly wish to have broadcast. The price Rob had to pay was only in words — the following humble words:

> *'... for as much as an noble Lord, John Lord Murray, is pleased to receive me into his Lordship's favour notwithstanding of my many ungrateful deportments and undecent carriages for some years by past ... the said Robert Roy Campbell, sometime McGregor, son to Lieut. Col. McGregor, shall hereafter and in all time coming, not only behave himself as a loyal and dutiful subject under this present government but also as an honest, faithful and obedient servant to the noble Lord and shall present himself to his Lordship when ever required.'*

Murray made up this peculiar statement, and Rob signed it of his own free will. Why? Many must have asked that question — but I have never heard any attempt at an answer. Perhaps I may be permitted to offer an answer of my own, on some little knowledge of the characters involved, the state of affairs in Scotland — and England too — at the time, and subsequent history?

I think it quite probable, in fact, that Rob himself was the instigator of the proceedings, not Murray. I think that Rob was indeed using the same methods that he did in his protection racket business, to deal with the threat of Murray and the Government. In the matter of the Watch and the cattle protection, this has been called by the unkind name of blackmail; I would hesitate to call it that, but I would suggest that Rob used some very real pressure on the Secretary of State to make him call off his campaign against him, and to cooperate instead. The Bond, I suggest, was merely a way of whitewashing it all, making it possible for Murray to agree to Rob's demands without a suspicious sacrifice of outward dignity.

If this is so, such pressure must have been powerful. What could a young Highlander of 25 years, not even a chieftain of a sept, member of a proscribed and persecuted clan, do, to bring His Majesty's Principal Secretary of State more or less to his knees? I think the answer may be found in what Rob knew. I think it is significant that those three witnesses to the Bond were, all in a few years time, to be active leaders in the Jacobite cause, as was Rob himself.

Is it too much to believe that Lord Murray, the powerful Whig Secretary of State, soon to be not only Earl of Tullibardine but created first Duke of Atholl, was in fact all the time secretly either a Jacobite sympathiser or prepared to be one if politically advantageous? That he was in secret touch with King James in France, while so prominently serving King William in London? If so, he was by no means the first to take such precautions. The Atholl family, after all, were half Stewarts; Stewart-Murray was and still is their name, and they were descended from the royal House of Stewart. As a family they were more Jacobite than otherwise, whatever the politics of the old Marquis and his eldest son Murray. The Secretary of State had a number of sons of his own, and most of them fought for the Stewarts in the subsequent two Risings, one of them being none other than the famous Lord George Murray, Prince Charlie's principal general. Another, the rightful second Duke, led the Clan Murray for the Pretender, and a third, Lord Charles, was sentenced to death after capture.

At this time, about 1695, the Jacobite cause was taking on a new hopefulness, after being in the doldrums for years. So much so that Dutch King William, who had no children, even suggested that after his death King James's son, the exiled Prince of Wales, should succeed to the throne. Moreover, a new group of Jacobite advisers were gaining power with James, called the Compounders — that is, compromisers, political moderates who urged new and less extreme policies on the former King which might well have gained enough popularity to have turned the people of England as well as Scotland back to his favour. The famous Test Act was to be respected; it required everyone who held office in Church or State to sign a declaration, very ambiguous in terms, that they would not seek to overturn the established Protestant religion. The Church of England was to be maintained, and all laws passed since the Revolution confirmed — thus banishing the bogey of the Stewarts trying to make Britain Catholic again, which was the main thing against them. So politicians in high places might well be doing some hard thinking about their futures, those in Scotland particularly.

In this connection it is interesting to note that a few years later, in 1703, Murray, by this time Duke of Atholl, was in fact openly accused of being involved in the abortive Jacobite scheme called 'The Scotch Plot or Conspiracy', and by no less a person than the same Simon Fraser, Lord Lovat, witness to that Bond, who was then acting as an emissary between the Old Pretender and his supporters in this country. Whether this accusation had any truth in it or not — for Lovat was an unscrupulous man and had become an enemy of

Atholl's — is not clear. But at any rate it was Rob Roy who gave evidence then to help clear Atholl's name — a strange situation. Atholl was forced, however, to give up his position in the Government.

How did Rob Roy come into all this intrigue and political manoeuvring? I have said that he was a confirmed Jacobite, like his father before him, but kept his politics under his bonnet. That is true, but though he did so secretly and very discreetly, he never ceased to work for a Stewart restoration. His mode of life made him a most suitable link between Jacobites, for he was always moving about the country, calling on lairds and landowners, attending fairs and markets and so on. What would have been suspicious activities on the part of most men, were his normal routine. He seems to have been a trusted courier and go-between from very early days, and as such was in a wonderful position to learn exactly what was going on in the secret world of political tug-o'-war. It is my guess that he discovered that Murray was making tentative approaches so as to be ready to change sides if necessary, and let Murray know that he knew, using his knowledge to force the Secretary of State to change the Government's entire attitude towards himself. I may be wrong, but I cannot think of any other situation that would account for this sudden and totally unlooked for compact between these two men.

At all events, for the time being the barometer was set fair for Rob Roy MacGregor. There are no accounts of trouble with the law or the Government — nor any of the Atholl estates having trouble with cattle-thieves either. The Watch went from strength to strength. Rob's cattle-dealing business spread and prospered, and he became a sort of cattle king in Scotland. He extended his droving and dealing activities far north into the remote West Highlands and Islands, and even down over the Border into England. And all this time he was carrying messages, orders, plans, between King James's scattered supporters, as gradually the Jacobite cause grew strong again.

In those five years Rob Roy's peace and prosperity grew to be almost a trial to him — for he was of course a man who loved adventure, stirring doings and the clash of temperament and arms. But he could console himself that the time was coming when the Stewart cause must be put to the test — and then, undoubtedly, there would be adventure and clash to spare!

Strangely enough, the very success of his efforts to bring the rule of his own kind of law and order to the important and hitherto ever-troubled area where Highlands and Lowlands met, produced its own problems, requiring something of a return to vigorous action for a while. What happened was that, as months and years passed without any thefts of cattle occurring, thanks to Rob's effective system, a small number of lairds and farmers began to feel that they were paying their protection money for nothing. Here and there, therefore, individuals began to default on their payments. A foolish but perhaps not unnatural reaction. I suppose that there are still people who stop paying their fire insurance premiums because they have never actually seen their house on fire.

Rob was annoyed — but at the same time almost gleeful. It became necessary to teach such shortsighted folk a lesson. Sudden outbreaks of cattle-lifting shook the countryside once again, and on a major scale. It was not just a few beasts that were apt to be involved, but the entire stock of sundry lairds disappeared overnight — usually of people who had omitted to renew their subscriptions to the Glengyle Watch. Angry complaints to the authorities produced only polite condolences. It was not long, however, before simple arithmetic triumphed over both indignation and pride, and Rob Roy's services were recognised once more as well worth paying for.

CHAPTER 5

The White Bull of Gallangad

A NUMBER of circumstances brought those, the most peaceful, easy and prosperously uneventful five years of Rob Roy's life, to an end. These were, in fact, mainly the deaths of various people. His elder brother John, Glengyle, died in 1700. The exiled King James died in 1700. William of Orange, King in London, died in 1702. And Hugh MacGregor, the only surviving son of Kilmanan, high chief of Clan Alpine, died soon afterwards. All these deaths had a marked effect on Rob's career.

The unexpected death of his brother, at a comparatively early age, threw a great new responsibility on to Rob's shoulders. John had left two young sons, the elder of which, Gregor, aged 11, became Glengyle in his turn. Rob therefore was not the new chieftain of Clan Dougal Ciar, but he became its leader inevitably in practice, responsible to his nephew. The clan system had a name for this situation, when an older relative became the effective leader during the minority of a young chief: he was called the Tutor. So Rob became Tutor of Glengyle.

Needless to say, Tutor in this connection had a vastly different meaning from that in normal English usage, for it meant taking on all the responsibilities of chieftainship, as father, captain, judge, adviser and governor to the entire clan. But in this instance Rob voluntarily took on the other kind of tutorship also. He was very fond of his young nephew Gregor, and also of his widowed sister-in-law Christian, Lady Glengyle. So he took these two, and also of course the two younger children, Donald and Catherine, very much under his wing. Now he was a busy man indeed. As well as running his ever-growing business, captaining the Watch, factoring Kilmanan's estates for him, looking after the destinies of Clan Dougal Ciar, he was managing the Glengyle property for his sister-in-law and bringing up his nephew as a Highland chieftain should be reared. Moreover, he was involving himself ever deeper in Jacobite affairs.

A Highland chieftain had very great responsibilities and duties, as well as power and privileges. It was not just a case of swaggering about at the head of some hundreds of armed clansmen. He was the patriarch of his clan, with complete hereditary jurisdiction over his people, with the power of pit and gallows, of life and death and imprisonment, like any Lowland baron. But he was also expected to be the friend and adviser of all. Every clansman had the right to approach his chief at any time, and was apt to name him as cousin. The clan's land was all in the chief's name, but it was always mainly farmed out to tacksmen, lesser lairds, who in turn saw that the ordinary clansmen were secure in their little holdings. There was usually a clan council, over which the chief presided, so that some sort of democratic government subsisted. Nevertheless the chief's word was law, and he need not take the advice of his council.

It all added up to a great deal of work for Rob Roy. The tutoring of Gregor Ghlun Dhu — or Black Knee, from a mole on the boy's left knee — both in the duties he would have to take on one day as chieftain, and in the more normal education which Rob was determined he should have in academic subjects as well as in swordcraft, horsemanship, hillcraft, manly sports and other suitable attributes of a Highland gentleman, took up much of his uncle's time. His own first son, Coll, was born that same year. It has been alleged with some truth that Rob Roy made a better job of bringing up his nephew than he did with his own sons, none of whom turned out to be wholly admirable characters. If there is anything in this, it is probably because Gregor was fortunate enough to have Rob's wholehearted attention at a time when he could best benefit by it. Later, when Rob's own sons were growing up, he was seldom at home, being deeply involved in the Jacobite campaigns.

The approach to these campaigns seemed to receive a serious set-back the following year when James II of Great Britain — and VII of Scotland — died in France, and King Louis XIV and most other European monarchs proclaimed his 13-year-old son, the Prince of Wales, as James III of Great Britain and VIII of Scotland. There was no doubt that a boy of 13 did not represent the same cause to fight for as a crowned mature king in exile. Plans for a rising were abruptly upset, then postponed. Jacobites argued amongst themselves what should be done now. Should attempts go ahead to put this boy on his father's throne as soon as possible, or should they wait until he was older, fit to lead a campaign in person and rouse his people — or until he possibly succeeded to the throne without dispute, when the childless King William died ? Much debate went on.

Then, before anybody was ready with final answers, in less than a year Dutch William himself fell off a horse, broke his collar-bone, and curiously enough died of it within a month.

The dynastic situation was now thoroughly difficult and confused. King James II and VII had been married twice. By his first marriage he had a surviving daughter, Anne, who was now a rather dull woman of 37 — so much older than his young son by his second marriage with the Princess Mary of Modena. Anne had been brought up in England, as a Protestant, away from her father who had, of course, turned Catholic. Queen Mary of Modena was a strong Catholic also, and had seen that her son was one likewise. Although it is likely that the Scots on the whole would have preferred to have young James as king, Catholic as he was, the English Tories were content that Anne was a Stewart, and thankful that she was a Protestant. They largely gave up their Jacobitism, therefore, and made common cause with the Whigs, whose Act of Settlement had already decided that Anne should succeed to the throne instead of her Catholic half-brother. Anne was therefore made Queen before the Scottish Jacobites could act.

The Scottish Parliament took longer to make up its mind, but under pressure agreed. It did have reservations, however, and presently it passed a measure called the Act of Security, which made it possible for the Scots, at the death of Queen Anne, to choose a different sovereign from the English, and thus revert to being a totally separate kingdom again. This caused much alarm in English government circles.

It might have been thought that now, with a true Stewart on the throne again, even though she was a remarkably unexciting female married to a Danish prince, and with the Pretender, as the Whigs called him, a mere boy, the Jacobite plots and intrigues would die down. But no — they grew more intense than ever. The reason for this was mainly political and economic rather than dynastic and religious. Since James VI of Scotland had succeeded to the throne of Queen Elizabeth of England, and had gone to live in London, uniting the two kingdoms, Scotland had begun to suffer the disadvantages of long-range government. Admittedly she still had her own Parliament in Edinburgh, but the King in London had great powers and still greater influence, and these were exercised through a succession of favourites and corrupt politicians. Royal direction and dominion was now 400 miles away. Moreover, the English, who had always been jealous of Scots trade over-seas, now began to take measures to filch this away. It must be remembered that for centuries England had been more or less at war with most of her European neighbours, and so not in any posi-tion to develop trade with them; Scotland, on the other hand, had always been closely linked with the Continent, particularly with the Low Countries and Sweden, and through the Auld Alliance, with France. Scotland's overseas trade had always been great for so small a nation. Now she was losing it because, more and more, government was being concentrated in England.

Things really boiled up to a crisis with what became known as the Darien Scheme. This was a most ambitious Scots colonial enterprise, organ-ised by that Scottish financial genius who founded the Bank of England, William Paterson, to exploit the Isthmus of Darien, or Panama, for trade and communications with the Pacific. The Scots people supported this scheme enthusiastically. Parliament gave its blessing, and the great enterprise was started in 1698. The expedition, however, quickly ran into difficulties — not the least of which was strong English opposition. Fever and disease broke out. The Spaniards attacked the colonists, claiming that the isthmus belonged to them. The settlers began to run short of provisions. Yet, though they appealed to neighbouring English colonies in the West Indies for help and food, on King William's orders no assistance was to be given. The English fleet in the Caribbean was to remain inactive.

The English authorities and English merchants had of course put obstacles in the way of the Scots colonists from the first — but this example of power politics within the newly United Kingdom shook Scotland. Indeed, at this very time, the English were actually refusing to allow Scots to trade with their colonies in America. It is all a most unpleasant tale of jealousy, greed and folly — an echo, probably, of the long centuries when English and Scots had fought each other over the Border. It all ended, unhappily, with the great scheme having to be abandoned, having cost Scotland 2000 lives and more than £200,000, a vast amount in those days.

It was in these conditions that the Jacobite cause grew in Scotland — more especially as the English were talking about uniting the Parliaments of the two countries in London. The years from 1702 to 1707 were full of intrigues, negotiations and preparations for what amounted to Scotland becoming an independent country once more. It was one of these, the so-called Scotch

Conspiracy of 1703 which I have already mentioned, in which the new Duke of Atholl, Lord Murray, was implicated by name if not in fact — an implication from which Rob Roy, significantly, was able to clear him. That Rob was in fact in such a position indicates that he was deep in the inner Jacobite councils himself.

I mentioned another death, that of Hugh MacGregor, Younger of Kilmanan, and that it greatly affected Rob Roy. Kilmanan himself had been going from bad to worse in drunken dissolution, with Rob, for the clan's sake, taking an ever greater responsibility. Now, with his only heir dead, Kilmanan seems to have gone to pieces entirely. He had got into hopeless financial trouble, and Rob had been advancing him money from time to time. Now Rob found himself a principal creditor to a bankrupt, as well as manager of the encumbered estates of Craigrostan and Inversnaid. Kilmanan had no further interest in anything — indeed he disappeared to Ireland shortly afterwards and was heard of no more. Craigrostan had to be sold up — and Rob, anxious to keep it MacGregor land, strategically placed as it was, bought it himself.

That he was now in a position to purchase this large property, indicates how far the penniless young second son had come in a few years. He was now a laird in his own right, MacGregor of Inversnaid, which was the name of the principal holding on the estate. He did not dispose of Monachyle Tuarach, but moved his little family from Balquhidder to Inversnaid on the east shore of Loch Lomond, which had a larger house and was more convenient for the governance of Clan Dougal Ciar and the care of his Glengyle dependents.

We get a revealing glimpse of Rob Roy at this important stage in his career, before warfare changed everything — and also of his nephew, Gregor Ghlun Dhu MacGregor of Glengyle at Lammas, the August quarter-day of 1706. These term-days were, and still are, the time for payment of agricultural debts and entry on possession of land in Scotland, and they were the days when Rob Roy received his payments for services rendered to the cattle-breeders of Central Scotland. On this occasion he was established, in the full panoply of a Highland laird, at the Kirk of Drymen, a little market-town — really only a Lowland village by southern standards — near the foot of Loch Lomond, sitting behind a table within the church doorway, at the receipt of custom, his Gregorach minions busy all around, handling the cattle coming in from all quarters.

Nine-tenths of all Rob's payments were made in cattle themselves, the most convenient method for all concerned in a country where money, actual cash, had always been scarce. Every laird and farmer whose herds had been protected — and that was considered to be practically everybody in some 750 square miles of fair Scotland — sent in some recognised percentage of his total stock, often coming in person to make the payment and receiving a handsome signed receipt from Rob, with drinks and hospitality for all at the local ale-house.

It must have been a stirring scene, noisy and colourful with a continuous succession of droves coming in from a wide area, lowing and protesting, dogs barking, men shouting, and bagpipes playing — for Rob liked to keep up a great style on these occasions, and was the soul of good-fellowship. There was something special about that day, too; young Gregor of Glengyle, now aged 17, was being initiated into his uncle's business as an active participant — and much enjoying the experience. As well he might; proud earls had contributed to his day's tribute — even the Marquis of Montrose, in line, it was whispered, for a dukedom; lairds of large acres and small, members of the Government, fine Lowland gentlemen and canny Highland drovers, the Church and State, were all represented at Drymen, acknowledging the power and influence of Rob Roy MacGregor, who might not be permitted by law to sign his name of MacGregor but whose word was more effective than that same law over much of the land.

All seems to have gone satisfactorily — for Rob, at least — until, fairly late in the day it was discovered that one of the lesser beneficiaries of the MacGregors' protection had not appreciated their services — or at least, had not yet come up with his due insurance premium. There was no tribute, either in gold, cattle, or even promissory note, from Graham of Gallangad.

Rob, when he heard, rose in righteous wrath — for all subscribers had had ample warning, and Gallangad was quite close at hand, a mere five miles south-west of Drymen. That its bonnet-laird should keep his betters waiting like this was insupportable. By the time that the sun was sinking, Rob's patience was at an end, and he declared that the foolish man must be taught a lesson. This was, of course, entirely necessary. A number of the Watch's clients, who had duly paid up, were still at Drymen, partaking of Rob's hospitality. No doubt they would make a night of it. Any sign of him letting off the defaulter lightly might well give them ideas as to the future. Rob had his reputation to keep up.

But in this same respect, there was a slight

complication. Gallangad was no proper laird, no substantial figure against whom Rob Roy could suitably pit himself. The term bonnet-laird meant merely a sort of yeoman farmer. While it was shocking that such a character should defy him, Rob would have demeaned himself by personally making any major move in retribution, as Captain of the Watch, Laird of Inversnaid and Craigrostan, and Tutor of Glengyle. Highland pride and business practice swung in delicate balance.

Rob found a way out by deputing young Gregor Black Knee to look after Gallangad's education on his behalf, for a change, the youth's first independent command, indeed, just as the Herriship of Kippen had been Rob's. Overjoyed, he seized the opportunity with both hands, and set off into the sunset with a few Gregorach gillies at his heels, in high spirits.

Gregor, at 17, was a fine handsome young giant. Fair-haired, ruddy, and of a pleasing, cheerful, uncomplicated nature. Indeed, history treats him well always — which is unusual in prominent men. Undoubtedly his was a much less intricate and involved character than Rob Roy's. Throughout his career, which was a long and active one, as a clan chieftain and soldier — he was Colonel of the important MacGregor Regiment throughout the hard-fought campaign of the Rising of 1745, and entrusted with many responsible tasks by the Jacobite leadership — I have read no ill comments upon him. Rob, all his eventful life, aroused mixed feelings — praise, fear, scorn and hatred; Gregor does not seem to have done so. Yet uncle and nephew remained great friends throughout 35 years of collaboration.

Gregor came to Gallangad as dusk was falling, and saw at once that there had been no attempt even to round up any cattle, or the sign of a move towards complying with Rob's demands. Not only so, but his request, at Graham's door, for some explanation was met only by a curt refusal, and that at the lips of a mere servant. Gallangad must have assumed that since Rob Roy had not come in person, and sent a mere boy, he could continue his defiance with impunity. Undoubtedly he was a bold if incautious and ill-mannered man.

History is silent as to the actual details of what followed. All that is recorded is that before dark that night, Gallangad did not have one remaining beast on his foothill grasslands. Every animal was on the long road to Inversnaid. Whether any broken heads were left behind in their place, we do not know.

What we do know is that in this wholesale sweep, a bull was included — a bull that became famous. For this brute seems to have been a tartar, and to have done as much droving as being driven. Had Gregor been more experienced, he might have left the bull alone but he was an enthusiast. It is a lengthy and rough road from Gallangad to Inversnaid by any route, but particularly by the way that Gregor chose, the shortest way actually, but certainly the way wherein he was least likely to be followed — across the marshes of the Endrick at the foot of Loch Lomond, through the Pass of Balmaha, and along the weary, difficult, steep and trackless eastern shore of the loch for 18 rock-strewn, slantwise miles. The Bull of Gallangad appears to have been in charge most of the way, and we can imagine a fine picture of the fierce Gregorach streaming on ahead, the cows and calves and cattle-beasts lumbering along behind, and in the rear the angry determined bull, roaring and snuffing and puffing in pursuit.

Even the most ferocious bull must tire, however, and that journey would have exhausted a
mountain goat. Before they were near Inversnaid,
it is reported the bull was like any lamb, a breathless and limp-legged lamb, and a child might
have scratched its ears, they said, and have led it
anywhere. Gregor MacGregor created a great
sensation by arriving at Inversnaid early in the
morning, before anybody could have looked for
him, with his great booty, in almost unbelievable
time for droving cattle nearly 25 miles over a
trackless wilderness. His reputation soared from
then on. How much of his success he attributed to
the bull is not clear.

Some years ago, I visited Gallangad, then still a
remote upland cattle-farm as it was 250 years ago.
I was surprised to find that the farmer knew nothing of Rob Roy or his connection with the place nor
did he seem in the least interested. It was only as I
was going away, somewhat crestfallen, that he
threw after me the jerked remark: 'Hey! D'you
mean yon bull? The White Bull o' Gallangad?' He
pronounced his bull to rhyme with gull, in typical
Lowland Scots country fashion, while I had given
it the more usual pronunciation. I hurried back,
agreeing.

However, that was all I got out of him. He
knew no more than that, it seemed — just a phrase
which had come down to him out of the past, 'The
White Bull of Gallangad'. No link with Rob Roy or
his nephew; no explanation of what the bull might
have done, or anything about it. Except this significant word: white. Though that bull has its niche in
history, nowhere have I seen its colour mentioned.
Here, the authentic voice of tradition, speaking
however faintly down the centuries, declared the
bull to have been white. Even Walter Scott, 150

years nearer the relevant date, had not been able to give his bull a colour.

CHAPTER 6

The King Across the Water

BUT now the dark clouds of strife and civil war began to bank up ominously on Scotland's horizon. The English Government and Parliament were determined that there should be an end to trouble with Scotland, once and for all. They wanted to incorporate it in a union with England, not merely as a united kingdom with the same monarch, but as one state under the same Parliament and Government, to make an end of the separate nation of Scotland — one of the oldest in Europe actually, which had already been a kingdom when England and France were mere groups of warring petty principalities.

The people of Scotland, needless to say, did not want any such thing — especially after the Darien Scheme and similar examples of rule from London. But the Scottish Whig leaders, including a great many of the nobles who depended on royal and government favours for their continued prosperity, were prepared to go at least halfway. They did not want Scotland to be swallowed up in England in what is called an incorporating union, but they were prepared to have a parliamentary union, so long as Scotland remained a separate country with its own laws, Church, and so on. This idea was most unpopular with the people, but negotiations with the nobles went on.

Actually, never had relations between England and Scotland been so bad, so bitter, as now, even in all the centuries of Border fighting. Possibly some in the London Government believed that the proposed union would help to heal this enmity; some of the Scots nobles also. Not all were actuated by hatred, prejudice and avarice. Nevertheless, debates in the English Parliament on the subject make just as unpleasant reading as does the correspondence of certain Scots lords selling their country for absurdly low prices.

On October 3rd, 1706, two months after Gregor MacGregor's epic of Gallangad, the Scottish Parliament met for the last time. It was a grim and angry session, sometimes almost degenerating into sword-fighting. It took three months to pass the Treaty of Union — and all that time Parliament House had to be guarded by soldiers against the angry Edinburgh crowds demonstrating outside. Many were the impassioned speeches made for Scotland's continued independence, but it was not a democratic assembly as we know it nowadays; the ordinary people had hardly any representation, and the Highlands had little or no voice at all. The great lords were grievously split on the subject — but sufficient were in favour to obtain a majority. The Treaty of Union was finally passed on January 16th, 1707, despite the Queen's Commissioner being stoned in the streets of Edinburgh, riots in Glasgow, and the Treaty being publicly burned in Dumfries.

The English attitude, official as well as popular, was that they had bought the Scots and could now do as they liked with them. Indeed, Harley, English Secretary of State, said in the House of Commons when Scots were objecting to the new Linen Tax being imposed upon them: 'Have we not bought the Scots, and did we not acquire the right to tax them?'

That there was a grain of truth in this, as far as the nobility is concerned, is revealed by the bribes paid to all the lords who would accept them, to vote for the union. It is extraordinary that men should sell their country in this way — but even more extraordinary that they should accept such paltry sums for their honour. We read that, of the nobles, Montrose got £200, Roxburghe £500, and Atholl (our old friend Murray) £1000. Of the Earls, Cromartie was paid £300, Balcarres £500, Dunmore £200, Glencairn £100, Seafield (the Lord Chancellor) £490, and Lord Banff only £11 2s. How these curiously fixed sums were worked out would be interesting to know; the Earl of Marchmont, for instance, got £1104 15s. 7d.

Now it was Scotland's turn to do the paying. Trade was taken away, goods had to be carried overseas only in English ships, new taxes were imposed, laws passed blatantly discriminating against the Scots, and hordes of minor English Government officers descended upon Scotland to enforce the flood of new regulations and orders, men specially recruited and often of the poorest type and loosest character. It was a current English joke that everyone could ride safely anywhere in the English countryside because all the highwaymen and cut-purses had gone north to rule the Scots.

Scotland seethed therefore, and the Jacobites would have been fools had they not taken advantage of it all.

Unfortunately for them, they were handi-
capped by one very grave liability — the character
of the exiled Stewart, King James III and VIII. He
was now 19, a somewhat depressed and depress-
ing youth, hesitant and melancholy, anything but
optimistic, highly unlike the usual run of the
Stewart men who, whatever else they may have
been, normally were a spirited and colourful lot.
James would set no heather on fire. When decisive
action was needed, he dithered. The Jacobites in
Scotland, with opportunity knocking at their door,
could get neither guidance nor real encourage-
ment from their King across the water. They particularly wanted the promised military and financial help from the King of France. No-one in
France, however, seemed to be terribly interested.

In all this turmoil Rob Roy was still involved,
but secretly. The first we actually hear of him coming out into the open was when an authoritative
envoy, Colonel Nathaniel Hooke, an Irishman, at
last arrived from France. He came through northern England disguised as a cattle drover, and Rob
was almost certainly concerned in this procedure.
He came to make preliminary arrangements for a
rising, and conducted a series of interviews with
groups of prominent Jacobite supporters up and
down the land. Whether Rob Roy helped to conduct Hooke around the country we can only sur-
mise, but he did help to organise the largest and
most important meeting of all, a 'tinchel' as it was
called — that is a great Highland hunting match —
at Kinloch Rannoch in northern Perthshire, in
Breadalbane's country, to be attended by most of
the Highland chiefs and north country lairds. Little
hunting was done at this colourful affair, but much
talking and some bargaining. Hooke eventually
got promises of support from the chiefs, mainly in

men, in their hundreds and thousands — but he himself was very circumspect about when King James would arrive to lead the attempt, and how many troops, ships, guns and French gold *louis* might be expected from the King of France. Eventually the usual Bond was signed by all present, pledging themselves to the cause, and asking King Louis to send at least 8000 regular troops. Rob Roy's signature appears amongst the rest, simply as 'Ro: MacGregor'. For once he had been able to drop the extra name of Campbell which the Government required him to use — for now he was defying the Government in something greater than words.

Thereafter the Jacobites waited and waited. No orders came from France to mobilise, no word of the King moving, of ships, guns or money forthcoming. The summer passed, then autumn, with Scotland in a ferment and conditions never more hopeful for a rising. Then it was winter, and no campaigning weather. The temperature dropped in more than the climate. Rob Roy was disgusted, and said so.

At least the delay allowed time for young Gregor of Glengyle to get married. He had fallen headlong in love with lovely Mary Hamilton of Bardowie. They were wed in that winter of waiting.

At last, in March, word reached Scotland that all was ready in France. King Louis' aid was not entirely disinterested, of course. There was an English army campaigning in Flanders under Marlborough, and the French gesture towards Scotland was as much to draw off this English threat to themselves as to aid the Stewart cause. Twelve battalions of troops were to embark in eight ships of the line at Dunkirk, the force was to be under the command of the Admiral Comte de Forbin, and King James was about to join it.

There was great excitement in Scotland. Rob and his nephew were very busy, acting as couriers to co-ordinate the mobilisation arrangements of the clan regiments and Lowland forces. They had their own MacGregor Regiment to raise, train and equip — although the training had in fact been going on quietly for a long time. To equip their men adequately, they both mortgaged their estates of Craigrostan and Glengyle. This move was not only to raise ready money to buy arms and ammunition, of course; Rob could probably have raised the funds otherwise. It was something of a precaution too, in the state that Scotland was in. If the rising failed, their estates would be likely to be forfeited anyway, in the usual manner.

It was not a bad idea to have them mortgaged to somebody reasonably sympathetic but who certainly would take no part in the hostilities, and who could therefore claim to be legal owner of the property if its true laird was forfeited — and possibly hand it back eventually to the original owner, by a special gentleman's agreement, at some later date when things would settle down again. Such an arrangement had the added advantage that if the rising was successful, the holder of the mortgage could then claim that what he had done was in the patriotic interest, and could hand back the estate to its rightful laird with a flourish, and so put himself in good odour with the new authorities.

For some time Rob had been working quietly with the Marquis of Montrose, who was a coming man in Scotland, and ambitious. He was of a very commercial mind, and indeed had actually invested some of his own money in Rob's cattle-dealing business. Now, with Atholl out of office and in the political shadows, and Breadalbane a committed Jacobite, although a slippery one, Montrose might well be the new power in Scotland; he was already Lord High Admiral, and a dukedom was just around the corner. Rob approached the Marquis about his mortgage, therefore, and Montrose co-operated.

Scotland rang with the slogan, 'King James, and No Union!' March slipped into April, and still no sign of the French, or of King James. Then word came at the beginning of May that the French fleet had sailed. Tension grew in Scotland, as men mobilised. Then another courier arrived. The French had put back to Dunkirk. King James had the measles.

The effect of this news on the mustering Jacobites, especially on the fiery clan chiefs, can be imagined. It would have been utterly laughable had it not been tragic also. What could be the fate of a cause led by a youth who had caught the measles as he set out to face his destiny — and then insisted on turning back, putting off the entire enterprise to have his measles in comparative comfort ashore? Rob Roy's comments, mercifully, are not recorded. The tidings were like a wave of cold water over the rising Jacobite hopes. Urgent messages, remonstrations and demands were sent post-haste to France. Things had gone much too far for turning back now. Large numbers of men were mobilised. The Government knew it all too well. If the rising was to fizzle out now, there would be serious repercussions and reprisals against those who were known to have mustered for the Stewarts.

These representations seem to have had their effect on James and his advisers. The French men-of-war, with an escort of frigates and lesser craft to the number of 30 vessels, set off from Dunkirk once more, with the King convalescent. It should not take many days to reach the shores of Scotland. Up and down the land men, government and Jacobite supporters, stood to arms again — the latter much more hopeful and indeed numerous than the former. The Government was, in fact, exceedingly weak in troops in Scotland, weak in support altogether, and weak in morale. The commander, the former General Leslie, now Earl of Leven, was almost prepared to throw in his hand.

Although the MacGregor Regiment — its true name was the Glengyle Regiment, since it was founded upon the nucleus of the Glengyle Highland Watch, and there were of course other MacGregors who were not connected with Clan Dougal Ciar — stood to arms with the others, waiting. Rob Roy strangely enough was not waiting with it; that was left to young Gregor. Rob was far away on a special mission, in fact. Two French officers had been sent by King James's headquarters at St. Germains as special envoys to those two great Highland chiefs of Skye, Sir Donald MacDonald of Sleat and MacLeod of MacLeod. These two, though Jacobite in sentiment, were luke-warm in the extreme, and had not attempted to bring out their clans for the rising. This was serious, for they were most influential with other island clans, and each could field perhaps a couple of thousand fighting men. So the French officers had been despatched to try to convince them, bringing money and promises of high honours and position in the new Scotland.

Unfortunately, however, owing to some mistake in navigation or other cause, the visitors had been landed not in Jacobite Skye but far south on

the Firth of Lorne, near Oban, in the heart of the
Duke of Argyll's Whig country. Argyll and his
main branch of Clan Campbell, unlike
Breadalbane, were strongly pro-government and
anti-Jacobite. The French envoys and their gold
were in dire danger. Rob Roy, as half a Campbell
himself, and as nimble in his wits as in his person,
was asked to go to the rescue.

It was a most hazardous business, for Argyll, a
veteran soldier, was very well-informed, being
high in the government service, and the Campbell
militia were mobilising all over his vast domains
against the Jacobite threat. Nothing could be done
for the Frenchmen by force; it had to be by stealth
and cunning. We have no clear details of Rob's
enterprise, exactly where and how he found the
missing envoys — who presumably had at least
escaped capture. All we know is that he successfully managed to extricate them from their difficulties, got them out of the Campbell country,
escorted them across the huge and desolate Moor
of Rannoch into Glen Coe, and there passed them
on to his friend MacIan. From here they could sail
in a small boat down Loch Leven, and across the
arm of the sea called Loch Linnhe to the Cameron
country, safe Jacobite territory and on the long
road to Skye. Whether they ever got to MacDonald
of Sleat or the MacLeod, is uncertain; neither of
these two great chiefs did, in the end, join the
active cause. But Rob, his duty done, turned for the
south and home, hurrying to place himself at the
head of his regiment.

He need not have hurried. The French expeditionary force got as far as the mouth of the Firth of
Forth by May 23rd, 1708. In Leith, the port of
Edinburgh, the government general, Lord Leven,
was preparing to abandon town and city with the

two or three regiments that he had to face the enemy, so alarmed was he at the situation, so confident that the Jacobites would be walking the streets. But an English naval squadron under Sir George Byng had trailed the Frenchmen north. Now it hove into sight, and worked into the mouth of the Forth behind Forbin. Some accounts say that it had kept pretty well behind because it was a much weaker force than the French one; others say that it was more powerful. A fairly circumstantial source gives the number of English ships as 28 all told. The French had more than 30 — but of course so much depends on the size and number of guns.

Not that it came to guns. The French admiral had never been very enthusiastic about this whole venture; in fact he had at first refused to lead it. Now he decided that he did not want to be cooped up in the Firth of Forth with the English fleet, whatever their relative size. He therefore took advantage of a favourable south-west wind to make a sudden veer round to the north and east, and slipped out into the open sea once more, turning his back on Edinburgh, on all Scotland. This before Byng could come to grips — though Byng was demonstrating no hurry to come to grips either.

Having once started running, Forbin went on running — northwards, allegedly towards Inverness. King James, passenger on the flagship, may have been no hero, but at least he had not expected this, and having come so far, desired at least to set foot on his own land. He pleaded that the admiral should turn, and do what he was sent to do — to no effect. He demanded to be set ashore and was refused. He requested then that he be given at least one small boat, and with one or two of those near to him to be allowed to row for the

Fife coast, only a mile or two off. To no avail. Forbin said that it was dangerous — which to this naval warrior was evidently sufficient excuse for doing nothing. His Majesty's royal person must not be endangered, and would not be, so long as he was in his care. In vain did James plead, here in plain sight of his own ancient realm. He even went down on his knees on the deck, it is said. The Comte de Forbin was adamant — at least at fleeing. He did not long sail northwards. When poor weather blew up, he decided that this was an excellent time to dodge the trailing English squadron. This presumably expected him to continue sailing north — so he put about in the rain squalls, and set full sail for the south. With his 30 ships, 6000 soldiers, his guns, ammunition and money, plus the helpless King James, he made a swift and highly successful voyage back to Dunkirk.

It is said that there was great rejoicing in France at the safe return of the expeditionary force with this absolute minimum of casualties. Not a shot had in fact been fired. In England there was equal joy. In Scotland there was complete bewilderment, almost disbelief, followed by black fury on the one hand and hysterical relief on the other. The assemblies of men dissolved, bold men abruptly became diffident, dumps of arms were hastily dispersed, and the clans slipped quietly back into their most remote heather.

The MacGregors' heather was not quite so remote as some; and Rob Roy's business did not permit him to remain hidden in it indefinitely.

CHAPTER 7

Ambush in Strathfillan

ALMOST overnight the entire situation in Scotland was changed. the uneasy balance which had prevailed in the political sphere was gone. The Government and its supporters were suddenly no longer afraid of the Jacobite threat — and all the fence-sitters, the wait-and-seers knew which side to take.

There was, however, no reign of terror, no major campaign of reprisals, by the authorities. They were not powerful enough for that, yet. The hatred and discontent with the Union was as strong as ever, and the Government feared to fan the flames by making actual martyrs of the leading Jacobites. They knew that the Stewart cause had received a severe blow, but its latent support was still very potent in the country, especially in the north and in the Highlands. There was little or nothing that they could do about the Highlands, secure behind their great barriers of mountains.

So the Government contented itself with making gestures against a few, and not too harsh gestures at that. A number of Lowland lords, who could be reached, were arrested and sent to

London to be confined in the Tower — including the Duke of Gordon, the Marquis of Huntly, half a dozen earls and a dozen lords. However, they were all released fairly soon, either on bail or for lack of evidence. A group of Stirlingshire lairds who had ridden with their followers towards Edinburgh to be ready to aid King James and his French force, were tried in the Scottish capital for high treason. Their trial failed, partly because of deficiencies in the Scots law of treason — which Parliament in London promptly set about amending — and partly for lack of anyone willing to witness against them. A not proven verdict was returned by the jury — which meant that they could not be proved guilty even though no-one believed them innocent.

Other prominent Jacobites were confined for the time being in fortresses up and down the land. As for Rob Roy and his MacGregors, they could hardly be molested so long as they remained in their mountain fastnesses — as with the other clansmen. It would have required a large-scale military campaign to penetrate and subdue even the nearer Highlands — and the Government was in no position to mount any such thing. Therefore against him, as against any other Highland chiefs to be brought to book, cunning had to be employed. In most cases it was quite impossible to lure the chiefs out of their remote glens, under any pretext. But Rob's case, as has been pointed out, was different, because of his business needs.

It was a little while before any move was made, no doubt to lull Rob into the feeling that he was reasonably safe, and that there was no actual evidence to link him with the pathetic events of May 23rd. For himself, Rob was going very cautiously about his affairs, cattle being as much in demand as ever. When the summons came, it arrived in an unexpected form. It was merely a polite request from the Earl of Leven, commander of the government forces, that if Rob would make it convenient, he would be glad if he would come and see him in Edinburgh the following week. Nothing from the civil power, the Secretary of State or the Lord Advocate.

This put Rob in a quandary. It might well be a trap — but it might not. It might be only a warning, or even an offer of which he could take advantage. To refuse to go could mean that the Government might take legal steps to outlaw him — as the MacGregors were still technically outlawed. This would greatly restrict his comings and goings on business, to say the least. And if the authorities had evidence to incriminate him, would they choose this peculiar way to proceeding against him? They might, of course and no doubt there was considerable argument one way and the other at Inversnaid on receipt of this summons. If Rob had one great weakness, however, it was his pride. He hated to appear to be afraid, not to meet a challenge. He declared that he would probably stand to lose more by refusing than by going. He was not going to risk other than himself, however. With only one gillie, he set out for Edinburgh.

It must have been with no little trepidation that Rob MacGregor, in due course, presented himself at the frowning gates of the great Castle of Edinburgh, Leven's headquarters, on its towering rock above the capital — and it would have been strange if his heart had not sunk a little within him when the massive doors clanged shut behind him, the same doors that had held his father prisoner for over two years. However, he kept his head high, surrendered his sword with dignity, and was presently escorted into the presence of the Commander-in-Chief himself.

The Earl of Leven, great-grandson of the famous General Leslie of the Civil War, was a professional soldier. He did not beat about the bush when he had Rob secure before him. No doubt the cunning part of the scheme had not been of his devising. A middle-aged straightforward man, he accused Robert Campbell of Inversnaid of giving aid and comfort to the Queen's enemies recently. Could he deny it?

Rob was a master of words, in English as in Gaelic, and was proceeding to make it clear that he had done nothing which could implicate him in the events of May 23rd, when Leven cut him short. That was not what he was being asked about, at the moment. Had he not had dealings earlier than that, with two French officers, unlawfully landed in this realm of Scotland, with a view to subverting the Queen's loyal subjects?

Rob did not answer for a moment or two, his mind racing. It was the affair of the French couriers mistakenly landed in Argyll's territory. He had believed that he had got away with that successfully. There might have been local rumours amongst the Campbells afterwards that Rob Roy MacGregor had been involved — for his notable red hair and peculiar physique were almost as famous as his reputation — but he did not believe that there was any actual evidence, proof of his participation in the business. He took the bold line.

'What two French officers, my lord? Where? And when? Can you name any two Frenchmen whom I am supposed to have met? Such Frenchmen as have approached our shores of late have taken care not to land, I do believe!'

Leven himself was at the disadvantage of not knowing the officers' names. But he had a card to play. He thought that Rob, if he set himself to search his mind, would probably be able to recollect the two Frenchmen and their names. To give him time and opportunity to do so he would provide him with accommodation in the castle overnight. And in the morning, an acquaintance of his would be brought in, who might assist Rob's memory — one MacDonald of Dalness.

While Rob, appalled, was considering the implications of this piece of news, he was marched off to a cell.

Rob had no illusions as to the seriousness of his position now. Dalness was a small property in the high hills just south of Glen Coe, and its laird was a connection of MacIan of Glencoe with whom, of course, the French couriers had been left, to be set on their further journey north to Skye. That a MacDonald should have turned traitor and informer was a bitter and totally unexpected blow. But he could, undoubtedly, witness that he had seen Rob Roy in the company of the Frenchmen — though surely that would damage the name of MacIan, his own chief? What lay behind this, Rob could not think. Could it be because he himself was half a Campbell? Using a Campbell name? That MacDonald of Dalness, like the other Glencoe MacDonalds, was so thirsting for vengeance on the whole race of Campbell over the massacre, that he had betrayed Rob out of blind hatred? It seemed the only solution.

From his cell, after some urgent thinking, Rob besought his jailer that his servant might be brought to minister to him, as was a gentleman's right. This presently was granted, and the gillie, one Alastair Roy MacGregor — not Macanleister on this occasion — was allowed in, although they were not left alone together. To the gillie Rob Roy gave lengthy and detailed instructions in the Gaelic — which, of course, the jailer could not understand — handed him a letter, also in Gaelic, and some money. Prisoners had to support themselves in captivity in those days, so this would not seem out-of-the-ordinary. Then he dismissed him.

The letter was to an officer in the Town Guard, a Highlander as were many of that body, and known to Rob. Without stating that he was in prison, or even in the city, he requested this officer to do him a service by sending a sergeant and 12 men to a certain address at a certain hour that night, not long before the town gates were shut. There need be nothing more done, no entry of the house or any unpleasantness; just to have the party arrive outside at this time, wait for a little, and then march off. Such action would be much appreciated by Rob Roy MacGregor; it was to give a fright to a man who had done him an injury. A silver piece or two completed the matter, so that all concerned should have a drink at Rob Roy's expense.

Rob was not a man whom any Highlander would wish to offend. The officer would not have to think twice about so innocent a request.

How Rob knew where MacDonald of Dalness was lodging is not reported. Probably he charged his gillie to find this out first, before approaching the officer. At any rate, Alastair Roy kept watch on the house in the Cowgate of Edinburgh that evening, and when MacDonald stepped out for a visit to a nearby ale-house the MacGregor slipped up to the door that he had left, knocked for the landlady, and after inquiring if Dalness lodged there, informed her that he was a friend of his, from his own country, and that he himself was getting out of town quickly. He said that she should advise MacDonald to do the same, for he had sure word that the Town Guard was coming for him, to arrest him in the Queen's name, at nine of the clock. If Dalness valued his life and freedom, he would not be in Edinburgh after the town gates shut at 10.

Rob banked on his knowledge of human nature. A man who could betray and inform on one of his own people, to the Lowlanders, would be sure to have a guilty conscience—and had quite possibly done other things which would make him dread arrest and questioning. Dalness, when he got back, gathered together his belongings and went to wait, standing back from a window of his lodging which looked up the Cowgate. When at nine o'clock precisely a strong picket of the Guard, with lanterns, muskets and pikes, came marching into view down the street, he delayed no longer, but bolted by the back door into the maze of narrow wynds that led down to the South Back Canongate, making for the West Port and the long road home to Argyllshire.

The Guard and their sergeant thereafter had a drink to Rob Roy's health, and returned to their quarters. There was no summons to the Governor's room of the Castle next morning for the prisoner, as promised. All day he waited. Towards the evening, Rob boldly sent a message to Lord Leven, requesting that the evidence against him be produced, for him to refute, or else that he be released forthwith after wrongful arrest. At the second time of demanding, he was conducted without comment to the castle gateway, denied any interview with Leven, given back his sword, and turned out into the night.

It was not long before he and Alastair Roy were hurrying out of the same West Port as Dalness had done the night before, heading in the same general direction, for home.

Legends innumerable have, of course, grown up around Rob Roy's name. The above story is vouched for in contemporary correspondence, however. Less well authenticated is another adventure where treachery played an important part, at this difficult period immediately after the premature rising. The fact that no confirmatory documentary evidence has been left for some of these traditional exploits by no means implies that they did not really happen — for many of them are highly unlikely ever to have found their way into official records of any sort, and the people involved were not apt to write about them. James Hogg, the Ettrick Shepherd, writing less than a century later, recounts this hearsay tale as true — and certainly it matches well the circumstances and characters implicated.

John Campbell, 11th of Glenorchy and first Earl of Breadalbane, was a remarkable man, of great gifts, but something of a slippery customer. The sort of man who was worth watching if things went wrong and they were now going very wrong indeed for the Jacobites. Not a few of them looked towards him, on his vast north Perthshire estates, a little distrustfully. It will be remembered that it had been on his land, at Kinloch Rannoch, that the famous hunting-match had been held about 18 months before, and the Bond of Association for the rising signed. That bond, in the Government's hands, would be as good as a noose round many noble and chiefly throats. Men suddenly remembered it, and began to question where this incriminating document might be.

Word of where it was came to Rob Roy in most alarming fashion. He had excellent channels of information, in the Highlands as elsewhere, and he learned that all this time the bond had been retained in Breadalbane's hands. Now, although he had not made any move to muster his own men for the ill-fated rising, he was being accused of Jacobite sympathies and passed over for suitable appointments in the rule of Scotland. He was therefore parting with the precious paper — sending it to the Privy Council, in fact, as the price of clearing himself of suspicion.

Rob thought fast. His own name was on that bond, and the names of many friends, men whom he had personally brought into the conspiracy. That parchment must somehow be kept from the authorities. On the other hand, Breadalbane was a very powerful figure in the area in which Rob lived and operated. Rob had adopted his name and put himself to some extent under his patronage. In his peculiar position, he badly needed a powerful man behind him, with Atholl now fallen by the wayside, and ill into the bargain, and Montrose, since the French business, acting exceedingly cool towards him. He did not want an open breach with Breadalbane just then.

Rob urgently, but secretly, set about obtaining vital information.

What he discovered was distressing. Breadalbane was indeed negotiating with the authorities, and was using as go-between his notorious clansman, Captain Campbell of Glenlyon; the same man who had been responsible for carrying out the orders for the massacre of Glencoe — and of course Rob's own mother's brother. Glenlyon, being a government officer, was in an excellent position to carry messages and documents

through the Highlands by military roads, to
Edinburgh and the south. Through his agency,
negotiations apparently had gone well for
Breadalbane, and the price agreed was satisfactory.
The bond itself was to be sent from Fort William,
army headquarters for a wide area, in the sure care
of the next strong military convoy going south.

It was a long and difficult journey, even by the
so-called military roads, through the Highlands
from Fort William to the beginning of the settled
Lowlands — 150 miles of steep hillside paths,
rushing torrents, high passes and lonely empty
moorland. All army personnel travelled by well-
defined routes therein, keeping to Campbell territory as far as possible, even though this entailed
long detours. avoiding known danger-spots,
always moving in large parties, heavily armed.
The military knew only too well that they were
hated interlopers in a hostile land.

Tyndrum, a scattered hamlet, an ale-house and
a small military outpost, lay under tall frowning
mountains at the head of Strathfillan on the Argyll-
Perthshire border, something over half-way on the
journey. Whether any army convoy travelled
south by way of the coast, by Ballachulish, Appin,
to the Pass of Brander and Loch Awe or, as was less
likely, along Loch Leven-side, through Glen Coe
and over the desolate Moor of Rannoch, it must
come this way, for at Tyndrum both routes met
again. Moreover, there was no other spot for the
night, for many miles on either side of it, where a
sizeable party could put up with safety.

Early on a dull, wet and misty autumn morning, therefore, a group of Gregorach might have
been observed — but only by the very keen-sight-
ed — moving like wraiths in the heather and rocks
of the steep hillside a couple of miles south-east of

Tyndrum. The place was famous, even though most men had long forgotten why. The name might have reminded them; Dalrigh, the Field of the King. There was nothing there now; certainly nothing like a field — but then it was not an agricultural field that was referred to. It was a battlefield, rather — though even that was a misnomer, for there was no room here for any true battle. The Ambush of the King would have better described it. Here the great King Robert the Bruce had been ambushed and defeated by a comparatively small body of Highlanders, MacDougalls of Lorne, 400 years before. The King had barely escaped with his life, hero as he was, leaving behind him his cloak and its shoulder-clasp, torn from him by a clansman, and a treasured memento of the MacDougalls ever since — the Brooch of Lorne. What was good enough to bring the great Bruce to his knees, was good enough for Rob Roy MacGregor.

Here the slender muddy drove road twisted and turned through a cleft of the hills just above the deep ravine of the rushing Fillan Water. As at Loch Lubnaig-side in Strathyre, men here could ride only two abreast. There was no way out of this long, narrow valley but onwards or backwards except for nimble mountaineers. Innumerable small burns, too, cascaded down the steep braeside from the high ground above to join the river, scoring deep red weals. The road crossed the multitude of these by a succession of narrow and roughly-built wooden bridges.

On certain of these bridges Rob's men had been busy, throughout the night. Now, in the dim light of this wet morning, they looked well enough; they would still carry a horse and rider. But a sudden jerk on a rope, attached to a kingpin beneath each, would bring them down in collapse into their respective gullies. Two MacGregors crouched beneath each bridge.

The rest of the band, about 30, were spread out amongst the outcropping rocks and heather clumps above the road, waiting, soaked to the skin, wrapped in their plaids, their horses hidden out of sight a mile away. Rob himself, with Gregor, was in a carefully selected spot near the far southern end of the defile.

The tired, cold and hungry men waited, silent and motionless. Their scouts had reported that 50 heavy cavalry horses had been tethered for the night outside the military post at Tyndrum. They thought now, enviously, of the dragoons lazing late this wet morning, snug in their blankets, or eating their breakfasts — and they told themselves grimly that he who laughed last, would laugh longest.

At length, when Rob had begun to worry about the mist and rain clearing, the listened-for signal of a curlew's high-pitched trilling call, thrice repeated, came from the higher ground in the direction of Tyndrum. The soldiers were on their way.

Presently Rob could hear the sound of hooves. Every now and again the beat of these rang a little hollow. That was the beasts trotting across one or other of the little bridges. Then figures loomed out of the eddying white mist wreaths below, which rose from the river.

Even though the dragoons did not know the significance of the name Dalrigh, and what once had happened there, they were trained soldiers and used to taking due precautions in this sort of territory. First came an advance party of six troopers under a corporal, riding in single file but keeping close together, eyes busy on the track ahead and on the slopes above. The muddy patches of the road had all been swept over with pine branches however, to brush away footprints, and the Gregorach themselves crouched low, well hidden behind the rocks and outcrops.

The advance guard passed on, unmolested and unsuspicious. There was an interval, and then more hoofbeats and the jingle of harness. The mist was thinning. Round the bend nearest to Rob trotted two troopers. Then a brief gap, and a single horseman. This man was enveloped in a long black travelling-cloak, but where his scarlet cuff projected towards the reins, gold braid gleamed. Also his cocked hat was gold-decked. Close behind trotted a non-commissioned officer. The main body, not yet in view, could be heard fairly near.

Rob had only moments in which to make his decision. This man was obviously an officer — but was he the commander? The man who would be carrying the precious despatches? With a troop of 50, there might be more than one officer. This one looked young, and no badges of rank showed beneath the cloak. It was a risk. And yet ...

Rob acted. He had chosen his own position with great care, at a spot where two of the steeply dropping tributary burns, little better than waterfalls, had dug their gullies quite close together, so that there were two little bridges spanning the track a bare 40 yards apart. As the second of the two troopers clattered across the second of the bridges, he raised his hand to one of the MacGregors who crouched under the timbers, watching. In a moment, just as the cloaked officer was riding up to it, the entire bridge disintegrated in front of him, the two kilted Gregorach darting and scrambling away in the gully, just in time to avoid the crash of the debris.

The officer's horse reared violently in fright as Rob jumped to his feet, two cocked pistols in his hands. As he leaped down, he fired one above his head as a signal, and then tossed it away. It was a bare dozen yards to the road.

That pistol-shot set the entire defile in pandemonium. Bridges collapsed behind and in front of startled riders, and all along the hillside above them great rocks and boulders, already loosened and poised, came crashing down. Men shouted, horses reared up and bagpipes skirled — the last always a terrifying sound for southerners.

The bridge behind the officer had gone only a few seconds after the one in front, effectively isolating him and the corporal at his back, from the rest of the company. But that company itself was also in process of being split up into little groups, separated from each other by suddenly yawning gaps, chasms and spouting torrents — always, of course, with the almost sheer drop to the river itself. With the rocks and debris hurtling down around them, nothing could have been more effective at throwing both riders and horses into panic and confusion.

In a few wild leaps Rob Roy was down beside the startled officer, who was vainly trying to control his prancing, curveting steed and at the same time tug out a pistol from within the folds of his cloak. At neither had he been remotely successful when his beast's bridle was grabbed, dragged round and down by a powerful and masterful arm, and a long-barrelled pistol thrust up within a foot or so of his face.

'Halt — in the King's name!' Rob ordered.

The other could only gape, and gasp incoherently, in a mixture of astonishment, indignation and alarm, most of his energies being concerned with staying on his horse.

The corporal had started to spur forward to his superior's aid, when the bridge at his back fell with a crash, and he had whirled round to stare. In two minds as to what to do now, after calming his own restive mount, he was making towards the officer again, drawing his sabre, when a fair-haired young giant of a man bounded down the slope and launched himself bodily through the air at him. Before his sword was fully out of its scabbard, Gregor's arms were around him, pinioning him, and then wrenching him right off his beast's back. Together the two men crashed to the road. Only a few seconds later the unfortunate corporal was rolling and bounding down the steep slope to the white-foaming Water of Fillan.

The two troopers who had crossed the bridge in front were now very fully occupied in trying to dodge a hail of rocks and stones coming down from the bank above them.

The young officer, after breathless shouts for help, recognised that he was not likely to obtain any at present. Also, that pistol barrel jabbing into his chest spoke eloquently. His cries faded away in gabbled protests that he was the Queen's messenger, demanding free passage in the Queen's name.

'Free passage you shall have, sir,' Rob assured him. 'All I require from you is a certain paper belonging to me and my friends, which you wrongfully carry. A single sheet of parchment — stolen property whatever. Give it to me, and you and yours may go unharmed.'

'No! No! Never!' the unhappy warrior cried. But as he stared around him, he perceived no aid coming his way. 'I ... I do not surrender my despatches save with my life, fellow!'

'With or without your life, it's all the same to me, sir,' the MacGregor assured him. 'But ... you are young to die for a piece of stolen paper!'

He observed how the other's hand went up involuntarily to his breast. Rob acted swiftly. Tearing off the man's cloak with a single savage jerk, a leather pouch was revealed to him, slung over the breast on a shoulder-belt. Another grab of Rob's long arm wrenched it off, all but pulling its owner out of his saddle with it.

Gregor came running up laughing loudly with joyful excitement. He took over the pistol, and the charge of the unhappy officer. Rob whipped open the sealed pouch. There were some letters inside but larger than any other was a long package from which came the unmistakable crackle of stiff parchment. Its florid seal — the arms of Breadalbane — undone in a moment, Rob had only partially to unfold it to assure himself that this was what he had come for. Thrusting other letters back into the pouch, he handed this up to the protesting officer, bowing.

'A thousand apologies for troubling you,' he said courteously. 'I wish you an excellent journey hereafter.' Reaching up, he took the other's pistol out of the belt beneath the cloak, and tossed it away down the bank. 'Good day to you, sir!' he said.

Rob and Gregor together raised their voices — and they both had quite excellent lungs. 'Gregalach! Gregalach!' they yelled, in unison, the slogan of their clan. As a signal to break off the engagement it was better than any pistol-shot, which might be lost amongst other shooting. Not that any shooting was in fact going on as yet; the MacGregors had their orders on the subject, and their victims were all much too busy at the moment.

The entire incident had occupied considerably less time than it takes to tell. As suddenly as it had begun, it ended, with kilted men streaming away uphill at the double, many of them laughing heartily. Two pipers still blew lustily further up the bank, parading back and forth. A shot or two did ring out now, from dragoons who felt the need to bolster up their morale. But pistol-shooting at long range is never to be taken seriously. Soon all the MacGregors were up with the pipers, vague figures melting into the morning mists. Rob waved the precious parchment over his head, and gestured away towards the hidden garrons. A few moments later not a soul was to be seen above the gapped and stone-littered road. Many Jacobite loyalists would sleep more easily of a night from then on.

CHAPTER 8

Outlawed

DESPITE these tactical successes, however, Rob Roy's lot was nothing like so happy as before the fiasco of the French 'invasion'. The same applied to all Jacobites — but Rob's position, although he avoided arrest and direct political action, grew steadily more difficult. For this he had to blame two men, one high-placed, the other low.

James Graham, Lord President of the Council, former Marquis of Montrose and now made a duke by Queen Anne, was ambitious and determined to reach higher position yet. He owned most of the lands flanking the Craigrostan and Glengyle properties to the south, and was seeking to extend them. As has been mentioned, Rob, always in need of a patron in high places, had adopted this chief of the family of Graham when Atholl fell from power, and Montrose had invested money in Rob's cattle-dealing business. Rob's brother John, indeed, had taken the name of Graham when Rob took Campbell, so that Gregor's legal surname was now Graham also. After the abortive rising of 1708, however, Montrose, who had sat skilfully on the fence, jumped down promptly on the Whig side, and was rewarded by being made Keeper of the Privy Seal. His attitude to Rob changed drastically. This would not have mattered so much had he not held the mortgage of Craigrostan and Inversnaid estates. Rob had of course spent a lot of money in arming and equipping the Glengyle Regiment, and business had necessarily been neglected during the long drawn-out preparations for the rising. Now he was distinctly short of ready cash. The Duke, however, demanded his money back, and with interest.

Rob, with a struggle, might just have been able to manage this. But it was at this stage that he was badly let down by the second man. I would not say that it was impossible that Montrose might have had a hand in this too. The man was one of Rob's own minions, not a clansman but one of his principal drovers, Duncan MacDonald by name, who seems to have managed the Monachyle Tuarach farm for Rob when he moved to Inversnaid. MacDonald was given the task of taking a special and extra large herd of Highland cattle south to the Lowland markets the following May. The country was in an unsettled state, but beef was in great demand. Rob spent every penny that he could raise and borrow on buying Highland beasts, to reap a great reward at the Lowland sales to pay off Montrose. Unfortunately he seems to have been prevented, for some reason, from supervising the droving and selling himself on this occasion — why, is not reported. At any rate, MacDonald took charge in his place and after selling the beasts for good prices, quietly disappeared with the money, all of it.

Rob was now in a most serious position. By

scraping together every penny, by using every method to raise money, legal and otherwise, he did manage to pay off the mortgage and free the estates. But now Montrose demanded back the money he had invested in the business venture also, plus interest. The fact that this was a mutual business proposition, and that the MacDonald theft was a business loss, made no difference to the Duke. He was in it to share the profits, not the losses. He took out a court order against Rob to have his former partner declared bankrupt.

This was a much grimmer development than it sounds. It must be remembered that the entire clan of MacGregor was proscribed already, legally proscribed. Any infringement of the law, therefore, by one of its members could have the gravest consequences. No legal safeguards whatever could be counted upon.

A date was fixed for public trial at Glasgow, but Rob did not attend. He has been blamed for this, of course, by some historians, as an act of folly if not an admission of guilt. I believe neither to be true. It seems to me that those who assert it are shutting their eyes to the real situation in which Rob found himself, and looking on the matter from the snug and secure viewpoint of present day legalities. Moreover, they perhaps overlook Montrose's character. The fact that he sent Rob a personal letter on the eve of the trial date, urging a meeting in Glasgow, and adding the promise of a safe-conduct, is surely significant. What Montrose wanted was almost certainly Rob's Craigrostan estate, which projected rather into his own great domains. He was always intensely land-hungry, always seeking to add to his broad acres. In court Rob would have been faced with this choice: either the debtor's prison, with all that it would mean to a proscribed MacGregor; or Craigrostan to be sold up, and of course taken over by Montrose, the principal creditor, as his own property. Rob undoubtedly valued his freedom above all else — but he also looked on his lands, settled now by his MacGregor clansmen, as much clan property as his own, in typical Highland fashion. Rob's pride was at stake in both respects. Instead of going to Glasgow, therefore, he went in the other direction — northwards, deeper into the inaccessible mountain wilds.

Now the gloves were off. An accused bankrupt had absconded. Rob was solemnly proclaimed an outlaw on October 3rd, 1712, and all Her Majesty's officers and magistrates instructed to seize him and his goods.

It was one thing to proclaim, and another to carry out, of course. People had tried to catch Rob Roy before, with no great success. But now there was this difference: he left behind not just a small rented farm in Balquhidder but a large and fairly valuable estate.

He went not so very far away, to a holding which he had leased from Breadalbane near the head of Glen Dochart — now marked on the map as Rob Roy's Castle — which is foolish, for it was never a castle and its true name was Corry-charmaig. It was a place useful to him for the assembly of droves of cattle from the Strathfillan, Glen Falloch and Glen Dochart areas of Breadalbane. As the crow flies, this was less than 20 miles north of Inversnaid — but over trackless mountains. Save with the help of Lord Breadalbane himself, it was practically impossible for the forces of either Montrose or the Government to reach it — and Rob, holding the famous Bond of Association and its story, had the means of keeping

Breadalbane quiet. His person therefore was safe enough — although his business could no longer be carried on as before.

What happened then is one of those terrible incidents which stain Scotland's history, however minor the scale. Rob has been blamed as well as pitied in this aspect of it. This time I feel that he did commit a grave error of judgment. He could not have been expected to foresee what actually happened — but surely he failed to take proper precautions for his wife and family; for he left them behind at Inversnaid when he removed himself to the north. Probably he did not believe that the Government or Montrose would war on women and children. Possibly he felt that, surrounded by his clansfolk, they were safe at Inversnaid, even though he was not. At any rate, on this occasion he failed in a husband's and father's first duty, to protect his wife and family.

Montrose was now so powerful that his factor, or principal land-agent, Graham of Killearn, was made Sheriff-Depute for the county — that is senior judge and law-officer combined. Strictly, Killearn came to Inversnaid not as factor for Montrose, but as representing the law and the State. He brought with him many constables and bailiffs to declare Rob's property of Craigrostan confiscated and to arrest his stock, belongings, and furnishings, as those of an outlaw. He did not dare to bring his posse through the MacGregors' mountains, of course, but sailed up Loch Lomond, arriving at Inversnaid one wintery November evening. Darkness helped to hide his approach, as well as the shame of his actions.

This is no place to recount how savagely and inhumanly he and his men assaulted and abused the helpless Mary MacGregor, making cruel sport of her afterwards. She was driven half-crazed, half-naked, with her three children, out of the burning Inversnaid House. All that could not be conveniently carried away was tossed into the flames. Killearn and his men returned whence they had come.

Presumably Gregor, only five miles away at Glen Gyle, and Mary's father and uncles only three miles off at Corryarklet, like the rest of Clan Dougal Ciar, heard nothing of the outrage until it was too late. At any rate, Killearn got clear away, in the name of the law. He was to pay dearly for his actions later on, however — as was Montrose himself. The Government, indeed, was to regret that night's work at Inversnaid.

CHAPTER 9

Revenge

NOW all was totally changed with Rob Roy MacGregor. His fury at the perpetrators of the outrage knew no bounds. His wife, each time he looked at her, seemed to reproach him. He saw all men pointing the finger of shame and scorn at him — the great Rob Roy MacGregor who could not protect his own nearest and dearest! From being a genial, friendly, dashing Highland gentleman, influential, however unorthodox in his methods, he became an angry, determined, embittered outlaw, something of a brigand indeed, his hand for ever against authority, thirsting for vengeance, the scourge of the settled Graham lands flanking the Highland Line.

Of course, his wrath was especially directed against Killearn and Montrose. The latter's great estates he now put under what amounted to a sort of reign of terror. Montrose had ruined him; he would now do his best to ruin Montrose, and at the same time make Montrose keep him. From his Highland fastnesses, with a band of the toughest Gregorach, he raided and raided. No longer was there a Glengyle Highland Watch to preserve the peace and protect the Lowland farms. Rob had now nothing to lose. His Mary, although living with him in Glen Dochart, was now a changed woman — cold and unhappy. Even to his young sons he was no longer the great hero of former days. He was injured where it hurt most, in his pride.

If it was the grimmest period of Rob's life, it was also the most active. His bitter hurt would not let him rest, and his temporary home held no happiness to keep him in it. He was determined to make Scotland realise that it still had Rob Roy to reckon with. I have no space here to recount in any detail his activities of the next three years. Whole books might be written about them. I can only summarise.

In the main, it was a personal campaign against Montrose and Killearn — he did not desire hurt to the actual tenants of the Duke's estates. So his activities usually took the form of uplifting what was the Duke's rather than the tenant's property. In those days, rent was quite frequently paid in kind rather than in money — grain, sheep, cattle, poultry. The Duke's factor or his minions could not get round all the hundreds of tenants at one time to collect these rentals, and it was indeed a prolonged process. Rob, therefore, perfected a system of collecting the rents before the factor could do so. This was plain robbery, of course but he was always most meticulous about the procedure, taking only the exact amount of the rent and giving his own receipt for it to the frightened tenants. These receipts were carefully, even elaborately worded, declaring that Rob Roy MacGregor of Inversnaid had uplifted on behalf of himself and his partner, his Grace the Duke of Montrose, the following amount, being full and legal rent for the said holding for whatever was the period.

Besides infuriating Killearn and Montrose, this placed them in a position of great difficulty. The matter was extremely awkward for them to rectify. The tenants in most cases just did not have the wherewithal to pay twice over. Killearn could curse and storm as he liked when he arrived — but that did not produce another rent payment, whether in money or goods. Rob, moreover, proclaimed it far and wide that any iniquitous attempt to double the exactions of rent would meet with the punishment it deserved. On the whole, the tenants were more afraid of Rob Roy than of the factor or the Duke.

Rob thought up an improved arrangement, better for all concerned — except Montrose. He approached the tenants to ask them if they believed their rents to be fair — for Montrose was a great rent-raiser and evictor. Needless to say, the alarmed tenants seldom claimed that they did. Whereupon Rob invited them to state what they did consider to be a fair rent. Then he would take this reduced amount — but give the tenant a receipt, in the Duke's name, for the full rent. Needless to say, this was apt to commend itself to the tenants.

Not that all of the tenants did lie down under the pressure, and co-operate. In one or two cases, groups of them banded together, possibly at the factor's instigation, and handed in their tribute, in grain, beasts and so on, at central assembly points well before the due date, for later collection by armed estate parties. But when these stores were raided by Rob's men, almost as soon as they were amassed and the entire tribute confiscated, and with no Rob Roy receipts for the tenants to show for their rents, they tended to have second thoughts.

Further to win over popular opinion, Rob began to use an ever greater proportion of the purloined rents to help the Duke's tenantry who were in need — and there was no lack of these. He lent and gave money and goods to those threatened with eviction, assisted the poor, the hungry and the unfortunate, and protected the weak. This had always been his habit — but now he did it on a large scale, looking for recipients of his bounty; and all at the Duke's expense! Before long he had the common people of a wide area almost on his side in this strange war; they were looking upon him as a benefactor against a hated and oppressive landlord.

A typical incident may be recounted briefly. A widow of the name of MacGregor tenanted a small farm near Balfron. She had had her rent abruptly raised to £20 Scots a year, and had not the money to pay. Rob's intelligence service was always excellent, and knowing that this was merely a preliminary to the woman's eviction, he came to Balfron secretly and gave her the necessary money. When Montrose's bailiffs arrived to evict her, she was able to surprise them by paying in full and demanding her receipt. A little later, however, the bailiffs themselves were waylaid by an armed party of fierce Highlanders and relieved of the exact sum, being sent off unhappily with a receipt of £20 Scots for the use of Rob Roy MacGregor.

So it went on. As the Duke and Killearn took every sort of precaution open to them, every evasive action, so Rob adjusted his tactics and defeated them. The entire countryside was in an uproar — but since Rob confined his private war almost entirely to the Montrose estates, other lairds and landowners found themselves distinctly amused, for Montrose was unpopular and overbearing. The

Government could do little or nothing, even though the Duke was Lord Privy Seal. Armed guards, even dragoons, were provided for the factor's parties — but since Rob operated against the source of supplies, the hundreds of small crofts, farms and hamlets over a huge area could not possibly be protected.

Gradually the success of his campaign, the constant action, and the gratitude of so many poor folk began to have a healing effect on Rob's bitterness. He began to enjoy life again. Indeed, he is reported to have declared to someone that he could hardly bear the Duke any malice after all, considering the amount of excellent sport he had provided.

But he did not relent one iota towards Graham of Killearn. That was a different matter. Killearn had shamefully outraged Mary MacGregor, and had to pay for it. Rob was forever leaving messages for the factor, warning him that his time would come. Graham never dared move abroad save under powerful armed guard, and what with one thing and another, his life must have become a misery for him.

Montrose, after many fruitless attempts to catch Rob, with companies of armed estate employees, volunteer militia from Glasgow, and eventually regular army troops, decided that as Rob always escaped into the trackless mountains where the soldiers dared not penetrate for lack of bases, such bases must be set up. He could not involve the Government in a full-scale war against one man, but he did get authority to establish one fort in the MacGregor area and one or two lesser outposts. Wisely enough, from his point of view, he chose to erect the fort at Inversnaid itself. Thus it could be provisioned and reinforced by boat from up Loch Lomond — and, sitting on his own ground, directly opposite the ruins of his own house, it would be a constant source of hurt to Rob's famous pride. An Edinburgh building contractor, Naysmith by name, was given the task of erecting the fort, and provided with an armed guard for his workers. His contract stipulated that the place must be ready for the garrison by the end of that year, 1713.

Throughout the erection of the fort there was no real trouble, nothing really to upset the builders or the soldiers. Then one snowy night late in December, when Naysmith himself had come from Edinburgh to inspect the more or less finished work prior to handing over to the Government, Rob struck. The guards, careless now after months of inaction, were decoyed away some distance by a ruse, and a lone traveller came knocking at the barred fort gateway, seeking shelter from the sleet. When the wicket-gate was opened, to inspect him, 30 armed Gregorach, hitherto hidden, burst in. The contractor and his workmen had no chance. They were expelled into the night, gunpowder charges placed in strategic positions throughout the building, and the entire fort blown up. The new bunks for the soldiers, just delivered, were piled up on to the burning building thereafter to make a bigger fire than even had blazed from Inversnaid House just across the Snaid Burn a year before. No doubt vengeance tasted sweet to Rob, as he slipped away into the dark hills illuminated by flickering flames that night.

It was not so easy to have the fort rebuilt. The contractor had lost enthusiasm, and workers were difficult to find now for such unpopular and dangerous work in the dreaded MacGregor country.

While the winter lasted, at least, the work was abandoned. Just when it was eventually completed and garrisoned, we do not know. At the start of the second Jacobite Rising, in 1715, it was not in use, whether this was because it still was not completed, or had been taken and again demolished by Rob, is uncertain. It is interesting to note that it was garrisoned and in good order 30 years later, in the succeeding Rising of 1745 — for it was in fact stormed and captured by one of Rob Roy's sons. Its ruins, now known as the Garrison of Inversnaid, are still there, on its knoll, above the rushing burn, with part of the buildings turned into a farmhouse.

I have no space to detail or even hint at the remainder of Rob Roy's stirring adventures during this outlaw period of just under three years. Suffice to say that he proved himself more than a match for both Montrose and the Government, and established such a dominance over much of Central Scotland that he was more feared and respected as a landless outlaw than he had ever been as Captain of the Watch, Laird of Inversnaid, and Tutor of Glengyle.

Only in one matter did he fail; he was unable to lay hands on the wily and cautious Graham of Killearn, who must have had his duties as principal factor enormously hampered by the ever-present threat of Rob's reprisals and revenge. Perhaps Rob did not actually try very hard to capture him; it may be that he recognised that he was making the man's life a pretty sheer misery anyway, and that the longer that went on before the final reckoning, the better.

But now more widespread and dangerous war clouds were once again banking up on Scotland's troubled skyline. Six months after the blowing up of Inversnaid Fort, in the summer of 1714, the rather feeble Queen Anne died, leaving no direct heir to succeed to the thrones of England and Scotland. Once more a king had to be found.

CHAPTER 10

The Sword Unsheathed

THERE were, of course, two contenders for the crown. James, still in France and already proclaimed by some to be James III and VIII, now a gloomy young man of 26; and George, Elector of Hanover, a distant cousin, son of the Electress Sophia who was a granddaughter of King James I and VI. Neither was much of a catch, as kings went — and George could not even speak English; indeed he had never learned to do so. He did not particularly want to be king, or even to leave Hanover. But he was a Protestant, and James was a Catholic. Under the Treaty of Union of 1707 it had been declared that if Queen Anne left no heir, the Electress Sophia of Hanover should succeed to the throne. Sophia died shortly before Anne, and the Privy Council in London decided to invite George to be king. There was great disappointment at this, amongst the English Tories as well as in Scotland, for Queen Anne was known to have hated George, and asserted to have left instructions that her brother James was to succeed her. However, George came, though apparently reluctantly, and James tarried in France. George had been hastily proclaimed king in Edinburgh on August 5th, 1714, Elsewhere in Scotland, however, particularly in the Highlands, James was also being proclaimed — even though he seemed to be in little hurry to stake his own claim.

So once again the plotting, the intriguing and secret arming began — and Rob Roy was one of the first to be involved. Now he was in a better position than ever to help the Jacobite cause, for he had little or nothing to lose, and he had his contacts everywhere. He did not have to be a secret Jacobite this time. We read of him drinking toasts to King James openly in Crieff town, outlaw as he was, before crowds at the cross, with the Town Guard looking on, in October. In February, 1715, we hear of him leading an attack on a customs official who had confiscated some Highlanders' smuggled brandy, before marching, with a great crowd of clansmen, pipes skirling, to the town cross once again, to lead three cheers for King James, while the brandy went round and round, no-one either wishing or daring to interfere.

But Rob was doing much more useful and effective work for the Jacobites than this sort of thing. £4000 at last arrived from James's headquarters in France to assist in the mobilisation of the clans for a rising, and it was Rob Roy who conveyed the gold safely to the chiefs. This may seem a relatively small sum today, but in those times, especially in the Highlands where gold was seldom seen, it represented a vast amount of money. Arms and ammunition were being smuggled into the country, and in this Rob and his MacGregors were very active. Couriers had to be escorted through hostile areas, and messages carried through the Highlands. In all this Rob was of the greatest use, and he now brought young Gregor of

Glengyle into the forefront of things again. The Glengyle Regiment was reformed, and everywhere the Highlands were stirring.

It has been suggested that Rob was not really a sincere Jacobite, and that his heart was not in this planned rising, after the debacle of the last one. Some historians and even Sir Walter Scott profess to see his later conduct at the Battle of Sheriffmuir as proof of this. I do not accept such an interpretation, and shall deal with Sheriffmuir later. Even though Rob had less to lose, those near and dear to him had, and yet he involved them deeply in the Jacobite cause. None doubted his love for his clan and for Gregor Black Knee his nephew: yet he committed both wholly to the enterprise. One of the authorities quoted as spreading the word that Rob was even playing a double game was none other than the ailing Duke of Atholl, our old friend and expert at double-dealing, Lord Murray, whose own sons were now turning Jacobite while he sought at all costs to retain the favour of the Government. None can rely on the word of such a man when he wrote to the Lord Justice Clerk that Rob Roy, he was sure, knew much of the (Jacobite) transactions in the Highlands, but that he believed that he imposed on both parties.

It looked, for long enough, as though this rising was going to be bedevilled by the same hopeless delays and hesitations on the part of James and his advisers as had been that of 1708. However, in the middle of 1715, a new star appeared upon the scene — John Erskine, Earl of Mar. His accession to the cause was unexpected indeed. Though a Tory, he had never been a Jacobite and had in fact supported Queen Anne, being Secretary of State at the time of her death. A Whig Government took over in London when George I was brought from

Hanover. Mar, though now out of office, was still anxious for preferment and position, for he too was an ambitious man. He went to Greenwich to welcome the new monarch as he came ashore and had the humiliation of being publicly snubbed, George rudely turning his back on him. Presumably somebody had poisoned the King's mind against him. Mar was both furious and grievously disappointed. He hurried back to Scotland, secretly — actually sailing as a deck-hand on a coal-boat to Fife, in most extraordinary and dramatic fashion — and startled Scotland by proclaiming himself for King James, urging immediate action. He called for a council of war, another tinchel or hunting-match to be held on his own lands in the Braes of Mar, to make the arrangements for a rising. At last things were moving, however doubtfully James, still in France, may have looked upon this belated and impetuous recruit. Mar had the nickname of Bobbing John — partly on account of his jerky gait, and partly because he was known to be something of a changer-of-sides.

Rob Roy was amongst the 26 Highland chiefs present at the famous gathering on the Braes of Mar on August 27th, 1715, with a great many Lowland noblemen and lairds. Mar was very much in charge of it all, although he was far from popular with most of those present, who doubted his new-found enthusiasm for Jacobitism. But he had the authority of a minister of the late Queen, and he was obviously prepared to commit himself to the attempt, prepared to act where so many in high position temporised. The Lowlanders would never serve under a Highland leader anyway, and Mar was the most experienced figure in politics amongst the Lowlanders present even though he had done no soldiering. The Duke of Berwick, half-brother to King James, who was a Marshal of France, was said to be the King's appointed Commander-in-Chief, and no doubt James would bring him when he at length landed in his ancient kingdom. Meanwhile, it was agreed that the Earl of Mar should be in control. The standard of revolt was to be raised in only a week's time.

So, at last, words and intrigues and plans gave place to action. On September 6th, the royal standard of the House of Stewart was unfurled amidst tremendous enthusiasm at Braemar, close to where the present Queen's castle at Balmoral now stands.

Scotland was grievously divided in this matter of loyalty. Still seething with discontent over the Union with England, her Protestant people were yet highly suspicious of the Catholic James as king. By and large, the Highlands and the north-eastern Lowlands, with some of Dumfriesshire and Galloway in the south-west, were for James, and rallied fairly well to his cause; the rest of the populous Lowlands, including the great cities of Edinburgh and Glasgow, plus the Campbell Highlands of Argyll, were for King George. In England, although there was some Jacobite sympathy, especially in the north-west, there was little real enthusiasm for a rising.

Rob and Gregor MacGregor were in it to the hilt, of course. Gregor hastened south to put the Glengyle Regiment on a war-footing and to man the strategic passes of Aberfoyle and Balmaha with 200 well-trained Gregorach fighting men. Rob went on a special mission to the Aberdeen district to raise a battalion there, based on a colony of MacGregors who had been established in the area nearly a century before by his grandfather, as part of a phase of clan warfare.

All over the north the clans were marching.

Success at first was with the Jacobites. But it took a little while to make an army out of the innumerable small clan and Lowland units, however good their fighting material. The Scots have always been a fiercely individualistic and independent race, difficult to unite in any enterprise. Mar had taken on no light task. It would have been different if King James's authoritative presence had been there to impose allegiance — but James still delayed.

The clans were divided by blood feuds and animosities stretching back over centuries. Their members would serve only under their own chiefs, and were quite as ready to come to blows with other clansmen as with the common enemy. MacDonalds from Glen Garry and Moidart would have nothing to do with Mackintoshes and Macphersons from Badenoch; Camerons from Lochaber were at permanent feud with the Frasers; MacLeans from the Isle of Mull looked with gravest suspicion at the MacNeils from the Isle of Barra, and so on. Units of 50 from some small clan were as fiercely proud as larger bodies, and would by no means be brigaded with, say 2000 MacDonalds.

Besides, the Lowlanders hated the Highlanders, and would not mix with them. They did not speak the same language even, each despising the other. Finding junior officers was not difficult, for this was a concentration of splendid guerilla warfare material; but senior officers, to command groups of the army, represented a headache indeed — for proud chiefs and nobles would serve under none but their own choice. The Jacobite army contained some of the best fighting men in the world — but the most difficult to regiment.

However, Mar did march out of the north

within two weeks of raising the standard — which must be accounted in his favour. On September 22nd, his advance guard took Perth, almost without opposition. Wisely, no doubt, he had not waited for the arrival of King James.

The government position in Scotland was very weak. London was in a panic, and refused to send troops north, fearing risings in England. Scotland was now being ruled by Montrose, as Secretary of State, with the Duke of Argyll as Commander-in-Chief. Argyll was an experienced and able soldier, a Major-General — but he had ridiculously few troops to hold down a restive country. His total force of regulars consisted of eight units: four regiments of infantry — the Buffs, the Devonshires, the Scots Fusiliers and the Edinburgh Regiment; and four of cavalry — the Scots Greys, the 6th Inniskillings, Carpenter's Dragoons, and Kerr's Dragoons. Altogether these amounted to fewer than 2000 men. There were irregular and militia forces scattered about the country, of course, but these were fit only to keep down the Jacobites of their own areas, if that. Red John of the Battles, as the Highlanders called John Campbell, Duke of Argyll, had an even more difficult task than had Mar. Moreover, his Scottish troops were scarcely to be trusted when it came to fighting their fellow-countrymen in a civil war.

In these circumstances, the Jacobites' obvious tactics were to strike hard and fast. But this is where Mar's lack of any military and warlike training failed miserably. He sat fast in Perth, waiting. He waited for King James and the Commander-in-Chief, the Duke of Berwick, to arrive; for reinforcements from the remote Western Highlands and Islands and South-west Scotland; for a sympathetic rising in England. He did send out skirmishing forces and sallies to Fife and Kinross and elsewhere. These minor operations were on the whole successful. But the main army, despite protests from the fiery Highlanders, remained inactive at Perth week after week, while internal jealousies and bickerings grew and grew. The Duke of Argyll dug himself in at the strategic town and river-crossing of Stirling, near where half the battles of Scotland have been fought. He must have sighed with relief, if not chuckled. Every day improved his chances and damaged those of the Jacobites — for reinforcements were on their way to him from Ireland and the Continent, and people all over the Lowlands were recovering from their startled fright at the rising.

Rob Roy, a born fighter and instinctive tactician, must have been appalled at the delay, for he was never a very patient man. But he himself was far from inactive at this time. He brought his Aberdeenshire recruits down to Perth, and then seems to have hurried back to his own countryside for a brief visit to Gregor and the Glengyle Regiment.

Gregor was still holding the passes, and thereby performing a most useful function, keeping Mar's back-door shut, as it were. But as well as this, he had been raiding around a bit, in typical MacGregor fashion, and we read that on September 27th, MacGregors under Glengyle attacked the Duke of Montrose's tenants a little above Aberfoyle, defeated them, and seized 20 or 30 guns.

This indication of Montrose's tenantry now being armed is thus explained. Argyll, at Stirling — a mere 20 miles from Glen Gyle and Inversnaid — was worried about his own left flank, as well he might be. He did the best that he could, encouraging the lairds of the area between Stirling and Glasgow, the Lennox as it is called, to muster their men and arm them at the Government's expense, seeking to establish a series of strong points facing the Highland Line. Gregor made a systematic assault on these places, using Rob's old methods and his famed information services. The favourite activity was to raid these selected strong points just as the loads of guns and ammunition from Argyll were arriving, and to confiscate the lot — thus both grievously discouraging the local defence levies and turning the Gregorach into the best armed units of the entire Jacobite army. Indeed Rob was soon in a position to do a profitable trade in selling cheap government arms to less enterprising leaders.

Rob, however, with only a day or two before he had to return to Mar's headquarters at Perth — for he seems to have been acting as a sort of aide-de-camp, leaving Gregor in command of the Glengyle Regiment — had a more ambitious operation of his own to carry out. This has been represented as a typically wild and individualistic exploit, picturesque but without real military significance, a mere Rob Roy-ish gesture. It was far from that. It was a carefully thought-out action, designed to weaken the left flank of Argyll's army, and to force him to draw away desperately needed troops from the Stirling vicinity. In this, no doubt, he was highly successful.

At dusk on September 29th, Rob took 70 of Gregor's men, and in a fleet of small boats set off down the loch from Inversnaid. Loch Lomond is 22 miles long, and though narrow at its head, at its foot it widens out to four miles. At this part, where it is well clear of the mountains and out into Lowland country within 12 miles of Glasgow, lies the large wooded island of Inchmurrin. Here the boats hove-to in the dark, assembled, and at midnight headed out purposefully towards the populous low-lying area south and east of the loch. This was all Graham country. The thought that Montrose's own home, Buchanan Castle, was a mere three miles away, may not have been wholly absent from Rob's mind.

For 70 men, the Gregorach seem to have made a prodigious impact that September night, and covered a lot of ground. It was not the intention to do major damage, to fight on any large scale, or to collect booty. The purpose was to spread the maximum of fear and chaos. In this Rob could hardly have been more successful. Soon church bells were ringing wild alarm over a wide area, and even the cannon of the fortress of Dumbarton Castle were shattering the night air. Certain historians have suggested that Rob Roy failed to surprise Dumbarton Castle, and had to content himself with terrorising the countryside. But this is surely ridiculous, for even Rob would never have attempted to capture the principal fortress in the West of Scotland with 70 men — or could possibly have held it had he done so. The object of the exercise was to create alarm and despondency, and so to force Argyll to weaken his position by detaching forces to the area.

The other objective now revealed itself. The MacGregors streamed back to Loch Lomond with the dawn, and split up, making in twos and threes for every little bay, beach and landing-place on the wide and populous loch-shore from Balloch to Balmaha, and from Rowardennan to Luss. Soon innumerable little convoys of boats began to head up the misty morning waters, each convoy consisting of one boat, lustily rowed by MacGregors, towing behind it a string of others, great and small. Every boat that would float around Loch Lomond was taken, and those which could not be moved were sunk or made useless. The entire boat-population then was towed away northwards to Inversnaid and the head of the loch, there to be dispersed and hidden. Rob had learned the lesson of Killearn and the Fort. With Gregor holding the entry passes, none could use the loch as a highway into Jacobite territory without somehow finding a vast number of boats. Moreover, all these stolen boats, waiting for Mar's troops, represented a new and dire threat to Argyll's left.

Rob was back at Perth next day, and was soon sent off to Fife and further local activities. It is worth mentioning at this stage what did happen later in this Loch Lomond affair. Argyll was forced to act, and it was no fault of Rob's that the Jacobites did not gain the full advantage of the situation, owing to Mar's chronic delays. A large government expedition was organised, taking two weeks to mount. On October 13th, Argyll was ready. He assembled quite an impressive force, mainly of militia and volunteers from Paisley and other towns of the West of Scotland, to add to those of Dumbarton and the Lennox generally. At Dumbarton itself the force was joined by 100 navy men, 'well-hearted and well-armed', from warships lying in the Clyde there. These brought their ships' boats with them, and dragged them up the River Leven to the foot of Loch Lomond. Here they were reinforced by Sir Humphrey Colquhoun of Luss and a contingent of his clan, inveterate enemies of the MacGregors, and the entire expedition set off up the loch. Part of a contemporary account of this colourful affair — from Rae's *History of the Rebellion* — is probably worth quoting:

*When the pinnaces and boats being once got
within the mouth of the loch, had spread their
sails, and the men on shore had ranged themselves in order, marching along the side of the
loch for scouring the coast, they made altogether so very fine an appearance as had never been
seen in that place before, and might have grati-
fied even a curious person. The men on shore
marched with the greatest order and alacrity —
the pinnaces on the water discharged their pat-
teraries* and the men their small arms, made so
very dreadful a noise through the multiplied
rebounding echoes of the vast mountains on
both sides of the loch, that perhaps there was
never a more lively resemblance of thunder.*

Having given such warning that they were
coming, it is hardly surprising that when they
reached Rowardennan they found nobody there to
confront them. They mounted the rocky bank of
the loch to the top of a hillock, and forming up as
well as they could, beat their drums for an hour in
noisy challenge. Nobody appearing, they went
down again, re-embarked and proceeded further
up the loch. Some accounts say they then went on
to Inversnaid itself, others say they went merely to
Craigrostan (which is a name for the whole great
property, of course, not a place), went ashore,
climbed another hill, and beat more drums, this
time also letting off artillery. No MacGregors forthcoming, they were departing when, by the merest
chance, they stumbled over some of the hidden
boats. Taking some of these in tow, and destroying
others, they set sail again down the loch, duty
done, announcing to the world that they had so

---

* Old gun for shooting with stones, pieces of iron, etc.

terrified the fierce MacGregors as to force them out
of their fastnesses and cause them to flee to the
general camp of Highlanders in Strathfillan. No
account indicates that a single MacGregor was
seen. What Argyll thought of this 'victory' is not
reported.

The mention of the general camp of the
Highlanders in Strathfillan — the same place
where Rob had recovered the Bond of Association
— refers to a new development. At last the waited-
for reinforcements from the North-west Highlands
had arrived. A large contingent of clansmen had
gathered from the remoter glens and islands, had
been marching south and had now reached west
Breadalbane. Under an experienced soldier,
General Gordon, they included the great chiefs
MacDonnell of Glengarry, the Captain of
Clanranald, and the veteran Sir John MacLean of
Duart, with large bodies of their men. At last, with
all this on his doorstep, the crafty Earl of Breadalbane was forced to commit himself. Reluctantly
he sent 400 Breadalbane Campbells to join King
James's army. Gregor of Glengyle, with his 200
highly-trained and experienced fighters, now
joined this corps, and was brigaded with MacIan
of Glencoe's MacDonalds.

Argyll must now have been an anxious man
indeed. Meanwhile, Rob Roy himself was in Fife,
where he seems to have been highly successful in
gathering in provisions, fodder, horses, arms and
recruits for the Jacobite army at Perth. He was the
ideal man for the task, of course even though he
himself believed that he could and should have
been better employed in attacking Argyll's thin red
line.

One or two diversions were being created from
Fife. Brigadier Mackintosh of Borlum, a very able

soldier, was detached to lead an expedition by boat across the Forth to Lothian, to try to threaten Edinburgh from the rear and if possible to link up with the Jacobite insurgents in the south of Scotland and north of England. This attempt was reasonably successful in itself, though it failed to surprise Edinburgh. The force did join up with the south-country Jacobites and eventually marched over the Border into England, getting as far as Preston, before it was stopped by government troops and forced to surrender. But though this did undoubtedly cause much alarm to the Hanoverians and authorities generally, it did not draw Argyll after it; it was a grave weakening of Mar's main force and served little good purpose. A more valuable exploit was the capture of a shipload of government arms, in the harbour of Burntisland in Fife, by the Master of Sinclair. Rob Roy is thought to have had a hand in this.

We know that Rob was back in Perth on October 14th, and had an interview with Mar, urging him to attack, and offering to guide an outflanking attempt on Stirling over and through the supposedly impassable morasses of the Flanders Moss through which he had driven those captured cattle after his first exploit at Buchlyvie, 24 years earlier. But Mar still put this off. He sent Rob instead as courier to General Gordon's Highland Division in Strathfillan, ordering it to make another diversion — not against Argyll's vulnerable west flank, but much further west still, to attack Inveraray town and castle, Argyll's own home, away on the sea loch of Fyne. This may have been an enjoyable episode for many who hated the Campbells — but it was another and most foolish weakening of the main effort, and a waste of time.

So October passed into November. King James

and the Duke of Berwick did not appear. Mar did not move. Argyll's reinforcements arrived from Ireland. Mar was now waiting for the Earl of Seaforth, the head of the great clan of Mackenzie, with the sub-clan of MacRae, which had belatedly taken the road south from far Wester Ross. These, with more MacDonalds, MacKinnons, Frasers and Chisholms, reached Perth early in November. At the same time, Gordon's Division from the west marched back from harried Inveraray and camped in the Perth vicinity also. Now the Jacobite army had probably reached its maximum strength of about 15,000 men. All were clamouring for action. Mar could delay no longer.

He wrote to General Gordon on November 4th, requesting him to send Rob Roy MacGregor to him immediately at Perth.

CHAPTER 11

What Happened at Sheriffmuir?

ROB at last had the orders that he wanted — but woefully delayed. He was to take the Glengyle Regiment, plus a company of Macphersons, and make his way secretly to that part of the great Flanders Moss across which he had declared he could lead an army. He was to reconnoitre its possibilities, especially in view of the heavy rains of that late autumn and the consequent high level of all rivers; if he found that a crossing was possible, he was to discover whether Argyll was guarding the outcomes from the Moss on the other side. If all was well, he was to send back information to Mar, post-haste.

Rob Roy had been pleading for action on these lines for weeks. Only a few men, all MacGregors, knew the secrets of the hidden causeways, fords and shallows of this vast waterlogged flood-plain of the River Forth. From time immemorial this had been the strange barrier between the settled Lowlands and the wild Highlands. Here even the conquering Romans were brought to a halt — although some of the underwater causeways were alleged to be of their making. This is what made

Stirling so vital a place in Scotland. It stood at the first point where the Firth of Forth narrowed sufficiently to be bridged — and to the west of it lay the quaking wilderness of the Moss, all the way to the Loch Lomond-side mountains.

Long the Gregorach had cherished the secret of how to cross this fearsome barrier. It had been of inestimable value to them in their raiding and cattle-lifting and warfare. Five miles across in the middle, its bogs and meres and lochans represented a most valuable trade secret. Now Rob was prepared to reveal the secret by conducting a Jacobite force across it, to take Argyll in the rear.

Even so, of course, it would be a most difficult and dangerous task. No ordinary army could have begun to attempt it. Cavalry was out of the question. Much of the crossing would have to be done in single-file, with men stepping carefully and precisely in the footsteps of those in front. Only Highlanders used to such terrain could be used. It would have to be done at night so that observers on the rising ground to the south did not see the assembling of men on the north side. In flood conditions it would be even more difficult. Even the approach to the area would have to be done in secret, for if word reached Argyll that any large body of men was approaching the northern flank of the Moss, he would almost certainly detach troops to watch all the southern rim of it, even though he could not know just where the crossing might be attempted.

So Rob's mission had to be very secret. This very fact was to tell grievously against him later.

On November 10th, when Mar broke up his long-standing camp at Perth and moved south on the road towards Stirling, halting at Auchterarder, the Glengyle Regiment moved off quietly south-westwards into the low foothills that lay between Strathearn and the valley of the Teith. Argyll had demolished the bridge over the Teith at Doune, and a secondary task for Rob was to find another suitable crossing of this river, on the way to the plain of Forth.

Most unfortunately no documentary evidence appears to exist as to what happened thereafter — though this is hardly surprising. We know that Rob and his Gregorach fulfilled their task of surveying the area, concentrating on that part of the Flanders Moss which centres round the Fords of Frew. We know that he was expecting a large body of Highland infantry to join him there and we know that no troops of any sort followed him at all. We know that he was away for more than 48 hours, with his own regiment — which, since the distance involved was a mere dozen miles or so, indicates that the MacGregors waited for a considerable time at the area of the crossing. We also know that Rob's reputation has never really recovered from the assertion, made not at the time but considerably later, that he deliberately absented himself and his men from the Battle of Sheriffmuir, and that when he did reach the scene, late in the day, he refused to take part.

It is here that Sir Walter Scott has been, I submit, most grievously unfair to Rob Roy. He states, both in his introduction to *Rob Roy*, and in his *Tales of a Grandfather*, that Rob's 'conduct during the insurrection of 1715 was very equivocal. His person and followers were in the Highland army but his heart seems to have been with the Duke of Argyll's. Yet the insurgents were constrained to trust to him as their only guide, when they marched from Perth towards Dunblane with a view of crossing the Forth at what are called the

Fords of Frew, and when they themselves said that he could not be relied upon. This movement to the westwards ... brought on the battle of Sheriffmuir.'

Scott was a novelist, of course, rather than a historian, and wrote this merely as an introduction to a novel. But the statement has been picked out and repeated by historians so often as to become accepted as true. It gives, in my opinion, a completely false picture of the situation. Indeed it is quite obviously inaccurate.

The insurgents, as Scott calls them, did not march from Perth towards Dunblane with a view to crossing the Fords of Frew, and therefore they did not trust Rob as their only guide. There was never any suggestion that the main army should or could take this extraordinary and dangerous route. Scott says nothing about Rob and the MacGregors being detached and sent away on their own with the task of surveying this route — and so does not make it clear why Rob and his men came late to the battle, a battle which Rob could have no idea was going to be fought at that time and place.

In the confused and confusing accounts of the battle, most of them compiled long afterwards, when the main objective seems to have been to whitewash the writers from all personal blame or reproach for a shocking defeat, it seems clear that the Duke of Argyll, learning that Mar had moved forward to Auchterarder, fewer than 20 miles from Stirling, decided on the bold course of taking the initiative and moved out from Stirling across the Forth, and marched towards Dunblane. This took place on November 12th, with Rob already away on his reconnaissance. Mar seems to have lost his head when he heard that the redoubtable Red John of the Battles was actually approaching him.

Instead of recognising that the proposed out-flanking move by the Flanders Moss would now be more valuable than ever, he cancelled the whole project, and decided to keep all his force together for a head-on clash with Argyll. The next morning, Sunday, November 13th, the two armies met on the slanting uplands of Sheriffmuir and fought one of the strangest battles in British history. A dozen miles away Rob and his MacGregors were still waiting for the Highland contingent to come to be led across the Fords of Frew.

That Rob, when he heard, did bring his tired men back to Sheriffmuir, even though they arrived fairly late in the day, seems never to have been recognised in his favour. That he would be utterly against the idea of a pitched battle with Argyll can be accepted, when the enemy could be so satisfactorily outflanked. All that is usually recounted is that when he did arrive late at the battle, he refused to fight. This accusation has stained his name indelibly and, I believe, most unjustly.

The Jacobites ought to have won the Battle of Sheriffmuir, even without the outflanking movement. Their numbers were far greater than Argyll's — some 15,000 against 5000; though, of course, the latter were regular troops against irregulars. Mar had the best position, also. In fact, the leadership failed grievously that day. But out of it all, the follies, the mistakes, the misfortunes and the disasters, only one man's character is really blackened — and that man is Rob Roy MacGregor, who had in fact so little to do with it.

Just at what hour of the day Rob and his MacGregors arrived in the vicinity of Sheriffmuir seems to be unknown. That it was after the battle had already been lost seems indisputable. Even Rob's keenest detractors quote the famous remark made to someone unspecified who urged him to throw his men in and try to stem the tide of defeat; 'No', he declared, 'if they cannot do it without me, they cannot do it with me.'

This brief sentence, quoted from an unidentified source and without its context, has been used to damn Rob Roy as a traitor ever since. The argument is that since no-one could ever accuse him of either cowardice or over-caution, he deliberately turned his back on his fellows in their need and disobeyed orders in doing so.

How true a picture does this give? Consider what Locheil the Younger, Colonel of the Cameron Regiment, wrote. His brigade had been on the Jacobite right wing which had at first shattered Argyll's left under General Witham and sent him fleeing all the way back to Stirling in the belief that the day was lost — but had then been rounded upon, cut up and broken hopelessly in their headlong pursuit, by Argyll's regular cavalry. Of the chaos that followed, Locheil says:

> *I rallied there all I could meet with, and caused such of them as had fired to charge their pieces. At the same time I perceived Rob Roy MacGregor on his march towards me, coming from the town of Doune, he not being at the engagement, with about two hundred and fifty, betweixt MacGregors and Macphersons.*

This makes it crystal clear that any picture of Rob standing idly by throughout the battle is sheer nonsense. The Highland right wing had won its battle, but in its over-enthusiastic pursuit had forgotten its flanks and suffered cutting up by Argyll's dragoons which had by this time defeated Mar's left, mainly irregular cavalry — all this before Rob came on the scene at all, marching from Doune on his way back from the Fords of Frew. The battle was in fact to all intents over. Mar's centre remained unbroken, but he held it inactive up on the high ground of the moor. His left had been shattered, and his right was in chaos after initial victory. With fatal indecision the Commander-in-Chief did nothing, it is reliably reported, all afternoon.

Another chief, Struan Robertson, Colonel of the Robertson Regiment, also on the right, says in his account that in the flight, as soon as they passed the Water of Allan, having met with a party of MacGregors going to join their army, they drew up and the enemy thought it proper to leave then.

This is not only confirmation that the Gregorach's arrival was too late to alter the issue, but indicates two other aspects of the matter. First, Rob's point of arrival in the battle area; second, the steadying effect of his regiment on the rout.

He, coming from Doune, reached the River Allan near Kinbuck, when he found himself involved in the broken and fleeing right wing of Mar's army, streaming and floundering as best they could across the swollen river. He could hardly fail grimly to recognise that these were the very troops which he should have been secretly smuggling across the Flanders Moss to get behind Argyll. Sheriffmuir itself lay a couple of miles away across the valley on the rising ground, and it was up there that Mar and the centre of his line waited, hesitant and inactive. So much for Mar sending orders to Rob to attack. Did Rob, in these circumstances, act mistakenly? I do not think that he did. He stood his regiment firm on the west side of Allan Water, like a rock in the flood of defeat, slowed up the flight, and saved the day, on this flank at least, from degenerating into a complete rout and massacre; for the victorious dragoons, chasing the fleeing Highland infantry, drew up at sight of a fresh and disciplined body of the dreaded Gregorach awaiting them on the other side, and dared not cross the river.

Should Rob Roy, instead of standing fast there, have led his 250 clansmen across the river in the face of Argyll's victorious dragoons — the very thing that they themselves were afraid to do, mounted as they were and in vastly greater numbers? I could not think of anything more foolish for a responsible commander to do. Crossing a flooded river in the face of the enemy is classically one of the most difficult military tasks, and when the enemy is more powerful and flushed with victory, it just is not to be considered. For Rob to have done it, with the battle already lost, might have won him undying glory — but it would have been sheer lunacy. It is in the light of this situation that we must consider his reported decision: 'No — if they cannot do it without me, they cannot do it with me.'

I believe that was the reasoned and reasonable decision of a very able and experienced guerilla fighter, seeing the military situation and summing it up. He had only 250 men. He could not change the course of the battle now. By standing fast he could keep the enemy cavalry at the far side of the river, and also tied there in case he in turn attempted a crossing, and at the same time give the broken Highland regiments the chance to straggle across and make good their escape, to reform. He did that.

For those who, because Rob Roy was a man in something of a mythical heroic mould, still hold that he should have done the heroic thing, however foolish and suicidal, for the sake of glory and his own reputation, I would point out another aspect of the matter — his intense loyalty and love for his Gregorach, his own clansmen. He was, after all, a Highland chieftain first and foremost, who reckoned his own people's welfare his first responsibility. He was a clansman first and a Jacobite second. Should he have condemned his famous Gregorach elite to certain annihilation for the sake of making a gesture? I think not. These men were his closest associates and friends, companions of innumerable frays — much more so than could be the case in other Highland regiments; they were, in fact, mainly veterans of his old Glengyle Highland Watch. He had never stinted their participation in the campaign to date. Should he have voluntarily thrown them to their deaths now, for the sake of an incompetent general who had tossed away every chance of victory — including Rob's own excellent scheme for turning Argyll's flank — and for a Stewart king who not only had never done anything for the Highlands but could not even come to be with the men who were fighting for him?

That Rob's decision was a carefully taken one, a judgment of the situation made intelligently and held firmly, is proved by the clash between him and one of his subordinates — although, strangely enough, Sir Walter Scott takes this further to prove Rob's cynical treachery. The detachment of Macphersons with Rob were under the immediate leadership of one Alexander Macpherson, a fellow cattle drover and associate of Rob's own. He was an impetuous man, and found standing still on the river bank much against his taste. Drawing his sword eventually he cried out, according to Scott: 'Let us endure this no longer. If he will not lead you, I will! '

Rob Roy replied coolly: 'Were the question one of driving Highland stots or kyloes (black cattle), Sandie, I would yield to your superior skill; but as it respects the leading of men, I must be allowed to be the better judge.'

Would any responsible commander have acted otherwise?

Rob has been further blamed in that, when the early November dusk fell and Argyll's forces fell back towards Stirling, he then did cross the river, following and harassing the retiring Hanoverians, and, it is claimed, plundering the baggage of both sides. This strikes me as on a par with the rest of Scott's criticisms — it shows a remarkable lack of appreciation of the true military situation. The issue of the campaign, as distinct from the battle, was far from decided. Mar's centre still sat up on the ridge, undefeated. Argyll was retiring towards his base at Stirling, not wishing his cavalry, his trump card, to be at a disadvantage in the darkness against the nimble Highland infantry whom the night would aid. It made excellent sense for the Gregorach to pursue now — indeed if all the other broken regiments had done the same, history might well have been written very differently. As to plunder, this was an accepted part of warfare in those days — and it must be remembered that the Highland troops were unpaid, and expected to make their own pay by plundering the enemy. The complaint that the Gregorach got much of the plunder seems to me a typical example of sour grapes on the part of those who were too busy going in the other direction to pursue the Government troops. As for robbing other Highland units' own baggage indiscriminately, this is obviously ridiculous. The Highlanders could not have had any baggage forward of the river. Their camp was back at Ardoch, five miles to the north. Any plunder which Rob's men may have gained, and which could conceivably be claimed by other Jacobites, must have been loot taken by them in their first chase of General Witham's fleeing divisions, and then abandoned when Argyll's cavalry turned the tables on their undisciplined pursuit.

I have dealt at length and in detail with this sorry story of Sheriffmuir and Rob's part therein, for in any attempt to portray Rob Roy, his life and character, this day's events are a vital matter. Obviously, not everyone will agree with my findings and conclusions. But if these will tend to make some look again and more deeply, into the question, and not just accept Sir Walter Scott's sweeping assertions, I shall be satisfied. Rob Roy was neither a saint nor a paragon of virtue, like the rest of us; but when a man's whole life is considered, his known character and general attitude to life taken into account, then commonly held views on the events of a single day, if they are quite contrary to all the rest, at least ought to be considered closely and with some attempt at understanding.

Sheriffmuir was not a clear-cut victory for Argyll. Indeed, from one point of view, the Jacobites could claim to be the victors, for they remained in possession of the battlefield, the Government troops going back to the security of Stirling, clearly uncertain of the tactical position and what was likely to happen next.

But in fact Sheriffmuir was the defeat of the Jacobite hopes. Mar's army never recovered from it, having lost all faith in their leader and their cause. The tide of war ebbed away after Sheriffmuir, just as the clans seeped away back into their own mountains. The Rising of 1715 was, to all intents and purposes, over.

Perhaps it is only fair to Sir Walter Scott to mention here that his doubts about Rob Roy's good faith in the Jacobite cause were almost certainly influenced by a very curious letter alleged to have been written by Rob more than 10 years later to General Wade, the terms of which were published in a book by an English officer, entitled *Letters from the North of Scotland* in 1818. This letter, if genuine, undoubtedly does not redound to Rob's credit, by present day standards of correspondence. In the matter of Sheriffmuir, however, I prefer to judge by his known character and actual behaviour. I shall deal with the letter when I reach the period of its writing.

CHAPTER 12

Divided Loyalties

IT took a few months to tidy up the loose ends of the Rising of 1715 — especially since, to the astonishment of all, King James himself turned up at Peterhead, north of Aberdeen, the day before Christmas. What made him come from France at this stage, months too late, without bringing reinforcements, munitions or money, without even the Duke of Berwick, is not known. He may have thought that he was being courageous — but he could do nothing useful. Nor was he of the temperament to inspire enthusiasm amongst his dejected supporters who nicknamed him Mr Melancholy. Nevertheless, until he sailed away again at the beginning of February, with Mar, now created a Duke for his services, the Rising could not be said to be officially over.

During that period of almost three months, Rob Roy, strangely enough, was perhaps the most active of any of the Jacobite commanders still in the field, more able and apparently willing, with his tight-knit, disciplined Gregorach, to tackle tasks the others were in no state nor mood to do — which gives the lie to any suggestion that Mar or other leaders, including the King, looked on him as in any way having let the side down at Sheriffmuir. The stories to that effect grew up later, in the main. We read of him in various activities for the cause — levying 'cess', or extra tax, on unfortunate towns and villages for King James, making raids to indicate that the Jacobites were still a force to be reckoned with, and generally showing the flag up and down the country.

Two interesting incidents preserved for us in correspondence, however, reveal that in all this military campaigning, he had not forgotten his private war with Montrose and Killearn. We read that he was in Drymen with 100 men on December 7th, marching through Montrose's estates of Buchanan, 'proclaiming the Pretender'. And again, on December 16th, he was back in the same home area, to teach a lesson to Sir Humphrey Colquhoun of Luss — who, it will be remembered, had joined the extraordinary boating expedition up to Inversnaid to beat drums and rival the thunder. It is not reported that Rob and his men did much damage on either of these two exploits; clearly he was only reminding his own home area that he was still a force to be reckoned with.

The most notable of Rob Roy's activities during these last expiring months of the Rising, was the curious little campaign in Fife. Jacobite headquarters were still at Perth, and Argyll evidently did not feel strong enough to make any head-on attack there. But Fife represented the Jacobites' weak left flank. Any move through Fife, of course, meant a sea-borne invasion across the Firth of Forth. Though a large area, Fife was fairly strongly Jacobite, and had been garrisoned by a mere 500 Atholl clansmen under young Lord George Murray, the Duke of Atholl's son, later to be Bonnie Prince

Charlie's famous general. It so happened that hard winter weather, which put an end to all normal campaigning, coincided with the belated arrival from the Continent of no fewer than 6000 government-hired mercenary troops, Brunswickers, Hessians, Prussians, and so on, the main reinforcements for which Argyll had been waiting in Stirling. These arrived in ships off the Fife coast early in January. Mar perceived that his time was now short. He had to move. But in order to allow King James and the Jacobites to move away northwards unmolested, he first sent Rob Roy and a few hundred Highlanders to reinforce Lord George in Fife.

For almost a month Fife was held, and Rob seems to have taken the most prominent part in the Jacobite activities — at least, his name keeps recurring in local histories, levying contributions at Falkland, foraging at Freuchie, and capturing and burning Balgonie Castle. The German mercenaries had been landed near Burntisland, and amongst other strong-points they were garrisoning this castle a dozen miles away. Rob attacked it with flair and complete success, marching off from the burning tower with about 100 officers and men as prisoners.

However, all this, though inspiring, could only delay the inevitable ending. The dwindling Jacobite forces marched from Perth on January 30th to Dundee, then to Montrose and finally to Aberdeen. Both King James and Mar left them before that, sailing back to France, and on February 6th, 1716, the sad remnants of a once great army were ordered to disperse quietly to their homes as best they could.

It was all over. The chiefs were advised to make formal submission to the Government as soon as possible. The Government, not being very strong or happy about Scotland, could be expected to be reasonably lenient if this was done quickly, not wishing to provoke any unnecessary hostility in Scotland, with the Union still so unpopular.

That was all very well for most of the Jacobite lords, chiefs and leaders. But not for Rob Roy MacGregor. He was still a civil outlaw, still bankrupt and nominally in debt to Montrose. He could not submit himself, without suffering the direst penalties. Montrose had no more forgotten him than Rob Montrose — and now that the war was over and Argyll, the commander-in-chief, no longer so important, Montrose, the Secretary of State, was supreme ruler in Scotland for King George. Whilst general orders went out to act mildly towards the late misguided insurgents and to accept the chiefs' submissions and so on, orders were also issued to apprehend and by all measures bring to book Robert Campbell, alias MacGregor, commonly called Rob Roy.

These orders had the result that the house which Rob had used as the home for his family during the campaign, at Auch near the head of Strathfillan, was burned down by a special force at the beginning of April, 1716. Although Rob was warned in time to get Mary and the children away, he does not seem to have been able to muster sufficient forces at short notice to prevent the large number of German mercenaries from wrecking the house and farm. Reports say, however, that he did manage to ambush the expedition, presumably afterwards, killing two or three and wounding about a dozen men. This was, it is believed, the last actual engagement of the 1715 Rising .

It was by no means the last of Rob's warlike engagements, of course — but thereafter they could not be excused or described as Jacobite military moves. It was just Rob Roy the outlaw and freebooter again. A week after Auch was burned, he led a daring reprisal raid on Montrose's lands in the Lennox, as far south as Duntreath, only a short distance from Killearn itself and less than a dozen miles from Glasgow. This was serving notice with a vengeance on Montrose that he still had Rob Roy to deal with. Moreover, it produced enough sheep and cattle to more than compensate for the losses at Auch.

Nevertheless, the situation was not the same as before the Rising. Now Gregor of Glengyle was being involved and all Clan Dougal Ciar. In government reprisals, Glengyle House itself was burned down, and no doubt the homes of many lesser MacGregors. It was one thing for Rob, the outlaw, to defy the authorities, but altogether another for Gregor and all the other settled members of the proscribed clan. Rob perceived that he could not go on using the MacGregor regiment for his own private feud without grievously harming those he cared for, and indeed the entire clan. But that did not mean that he was going to concede victory to Montrose. And he had not forgotten his personal account with Graham of Killearn. He made one of his sudden and typical changes of tactics. Urging Gregor to make the formal submission to the Government to disband the regiment and to return to as peaceful a life as was possible, he himself collected a tough group of volunteers, the hard core of his own fierce Gregorach, veterans of the Watch, and marched them away north by west, to Inveraray of the Campbells, the capital of the Duke of Argyll. When Montrose and Killearn heard of it, they must have been perplexed indeed — but probably heaved sighs of relief nevertheless.

The situation with regard to Argyll has to be explained. Despite the fact that Sheriffmuir had spelt the end of the Rising, his handling of the battle had done much harm to his military reputation. He was suspected by the Government of being too kind-hearted towards the rebels, especially the Highlanders. Indeed it is reported that during the battle, when he watched his cavalry cutting down the clansmen, he cried out: 'Oh, spare the poor blue bonnets!' A Highlander himself, even though a hated Campbell, the Duke undoubtedly was merciful after the collapse of the Rising.

Moreover, Marlborough, who was now ruling in London for King George, did not like him. He sent General Cadogan up as Argyll's second-in-command, but his real duty was to spy on him. Worst of all, Montrose was intensely jealous of him and of the great political power of the Campbells. As Secretary of State he was the supreme civil power, but in war the commander-in-chief was on top. Whenever the emergency was over, therefore, the Secretary of State reasserted himself, and used his great influence in London to bring down his rival. The Duke of Argyll, after having been feted in Edinburgh as the saviour of the country, was summoned down to London supposedly to receive the thanks of his grateful Hanoverian monarch. Instead he was dismissed as commander-in-chief and deprived of all other offices, General Cadogan being promoted in his place.

Disgraced and angry, Argyll came back to Inveraray a disillusioned man. Montrose had won.

Rob Roy required a strong patron more than ever. Breadalbane had had 400 men in the Jacobite army and was in disgrace. Atholl, whose sons had taken King James's side, was also under a cloud and a sick man. Montrose was Rob's inveterate enemy. Ever shrewd at manoeuvre, Rob saw his opportunity. Was he not called Campbell, and his mother a Campbell? Would this duke not look kindly on a man who was such a thorn in the side of that other duke, Montrose? Argyll might be out of favour now, but he was in a very different position from the others, a lifelong Whig of hitherto unimpeachable integrity, and head of the most powerful Whig clan in Scotland. So Rob took the road to Inveraray and put himself under the protection of MacCailean Mor, the Chief of Clan Campbell.

Here we get the first glimpses of intriguing questions that have never been satisfactorily answered, and some whiffs of the particularly dirty politics of the 18th century. Had Rob had earlier dealings with Argyll? Was Argyll, the noted Whig, a secret Jacobite sympathiser all the time? Was he possibly just a patriot who loved his country, and sought to pick his way through the mire of politics on both sides?

We shall probably never know. Scott had accused Rob Roy of treachery towards the Jacobite cause because, it was alleged, he had been in touch with Argyll, the Hanoverian commander-in-chief, throughout. If there was any truth in this — and Rob's letter of 10 years later to Wade seems to confirm it — then the possibility of Argyll's Jacobite sympathies puts an entirely different face on the matter. Rob's services to the Jacobite cause were innumerable, open and consistent. If he was in touch with Argyll throughout, then it is reasonable to believe that it was not to the detriment of the Jacobite cause. After all, would it be so strange if this Duke had divided loyalties? What of the Duke of Atholl, who had been Whig Secretary of State, who had been dismissed because of alleged implication in a Jacobite conspiracy, and whose sons were leaders in the Rising? What of the Earl of Breadalbane, who had been ready to buy Whig favour with the Bond of Association, but who produced 400 men for the rising? What of Montrose himself — who, when the 1708 Rising looked like coming off, advanced Rob money on a mortgage on Craigrostan estate, knowing the money was to buy arms, and the estate to be restored to Rob if the Rising succeeded? These were the divided loyalties of the times, while the Houses of Stewart, Orange and Hanover tugged for the throne.

Whether or not Rob had had previous dealings with Argyll, the Duke did in fact receive him favourably. Rob's interpretation of the situation proved both accurate and justified. Smarting under Montrose's perfidy and spleen, Argyll was glad to give shelter and protection to so noted a bugbear of the Secretary of State. Certain formalities had to be gone through first, of course. Rob had to make the required formal submission to a nominee of the Government. This was done to Colonel Campbell of Finnab, one of Argyll's lairds who was in command of the Independent Company of Militia in the Inveraray area — actually an old acquaintance and sparring-partner of Rob's. He had to surrender the arms of his band — but this was got over satisfactorily by handing over a rusty collection of old guns and swords sufficient to comply with regulations — keeping, of course, their own bristling array of well-used arms.

Rob could now be accepted by Argyll — who presumably did not take the old outlawry sentence of 1712 very seriously. Montrose did, of course, and was soon protesting to London about Argyll's infamous behaviour. It was one thing for London, however, to deprive a government commander of his appointment, and altogether another to make any impression of the great Duke of Argyll in his own country. Rob was given the use of a small farm in Glen Shira, a few miles from Inveraray, less than 20 miles from the head of Loch Lomond, and there he brought Mary and the children. Nobody, however, imagined that he had gone there to retire.

Montrose did not remain inactive, either. A military expedition was mounted on quite a large scale, with dragoons from Glasgow and grenadiers from Stirling, to clean out the nests of insurgents lingering about the head of Loch Lomond. This brought fire and sword to Craigrostan and Inversnaid once more, but failing to bring Rob and his men to battle, it had to content itself with setting fire a second time to Inversnaid House — which presumably Rob had had rebuilt — and beginning the restoration of Inversnaid Fort across the burn. We read that Graham of Killearn, in his capacity of Sheriff-Depute, ventured north into the wilds on this occasion with a strong body of militia — so he must have come to believe that the personal threat of Rob Roy was now more or less a thing of the past. He was to learn otherwise.

CHAPTER 13

An Old Score Strangely Settled

T HE military raid on Inversnaid had been in October. There had been no sign of Rob Roy since then in his own district. It was rumoured that he was much dejected by the failure of all that he had worked for, even that he had left Scotland for Ireland. Killearn was sufficiently encouraged by events, or the lack of them, to take a leading part once more in the important business of collecting his master's rents the following month, at the November term.

After a busy day on that Martinmas evening of 1716, Killearn was settled at the inn at Chapellaroch, some four miles south of the pass of Aberfoyle on the edge of the Flanders Moss. He only concerned himself with the collection of actual cash, leaving the uplifting of cattle and grain to his subordinates. Now, his guards outside, in the company of a number of the more substantial tenants of the district, he sat at table, dispensing Montrose's hospitality in the form of a good dinner. It was a cosy and comfortable scene, in contrast to the blustering November night beyond.

Suddenly there was the noise of a commotion

outside. Killearn was a cautious man in business matters. Whatever the bother was out there, his guards would deal with it — but nevertheless it behoved him to look well after the Duke's money which he had so successfully collected. This amounted to more than £3000 Scots, a very large sum for those days. Hastily Killearn ran with the money bags to the step-ladder which led up to the loft of the single-storey building, and threw the cash up there, out of sight, as a precaution. He was making for the door of the inn to discover what the to-do was about, when it was burst open and the feared figure of Rob Roy MacGregor, in dripping tartans, stood framed in the doorway, backed by a solid phalanx of armed Gregorach. There was no sign of the factor's guard.

Absolute silence prevailed in the inn parlour for moments on end as the two men confronted each other. They had not actually met for many years, although neither had for long been out of the other's mind. The farmers sat, appalled.

Rob spoke first, quietly, courteously at his most formal, not even glancing at Killearn now. He gave the unhappy tenantry good evening, asked their pardon for interrupting their repast, and urged them to continue with it. Afterwards he would have just a quiet word or two with His Grace's factor, with whom he had some business. The Gregorach fighting-men slipped behind him to take up strategic positions all round the room, as he spoke.

Never did men feel less like completing their meal. But Rob insisted, declaring that the Duke would be desolate if his guests did not do justice to his hospitality. The silent MacGregors stood watching. Hastily the tenants gulped some of the food down, eyes flickering from the table to each other, but never to Rob or his men, or even to Killearn, who sat apart, biting his lips. Quickly they made pretence of eating as much as they could, then got up from the table, all making for the door. They had receipts for their rents in their pockets, and were more than anxious to get away before they might be further involved. One by one Rob bade them a civil good night.

When only the Gregorach and Killearn remained, Rob signed to his men to sit down and finish the remains of the meal, while he himself turned to the factor, in calm and businesslike fashion. He reached over and took the ledgers lying beside Killearn, glancing over the figures.

'First of all,' he said, 'for my business with the Duke. How have the rents been coming in?'

Graham of Killearn tried desperately to bluff it out, claiming that as yet no rents had actually been collected. But Rob cut him short, pointing out that Montrose was not the man to pay for dinner for his tenants before he had received their rents. He thereupon ordered his men to search the house, and very quickly the money was discovered hidden in the loft.

Having added up the columns in the ledgers, and checked it with the cash in the bags and found it correct, Rob handed the money over to one of his henchmen, and wrote out a careful receipt for the full amount. This, he told Killearn, would be something on account for the Duke's total indebtedness to himself, including a modest assessment of the cost of burning two of his houses and doing much damage to his stock and properties. On the credit side, of course, he would include various of his own upliftings of Montrose's cattle, gear and so on. All must be done in order. By his calculation however, this still left the Duke owing him a tidy sum — at least another £3000 — but this receipt would serve for the present payment on account. When the rest was duly paid to him, then no doubt the Duke and himself could resume normal gentlemanly relations as between neighbours. He passed over the receipt to the factor.

Killearn did not know whether to bluster or sit quiet. His hopes must have risen that this might after all be all that Rob was demanding just now — that he was only interested in money and plunder. But his hopes were dashed. Rob, raising his eyes to consider the other directly now, said that he had private business to transact with Mr Graham of Killearn. It was not suitable nor convenient to discuss this here, however. He must ask Killearn to accompany him forthwith. He was sorry — they might have some little distance to travel.

Protest as he would, the now desperately alarmed factor was bundled outside into the night, and in the midst of a tight group of grim-faced Highlanders, forced along the road from Chapellaroch, northwards. No attempt was made to rescue him, even to watch him go by, on the part of his guard or anyone else.

The first night's experiences must have been terrifying enough for Killearn. The route from Chapellaroch into the heart of the MacGregor country was rough and dangerous enough at any time particularly for one not used to travelling through the mountains; but for a soft-living middle-aged man, in the dark of a wild winter's night, it must have been desperate indeed. By the shortest route, to Portanellan, the Harbour of the Island, on the north shore of Loch Katrine, by Aberfoyle, over the hills by what is now called the Duke's Road to Loch Achray in the Trossachs, and then north-west through the forest and along the steep boulder-strewn north shore of Katrine itself, is well over 20 harsh and difficult miles. How long it took the Gregorach to get Killearn over these miles we do not know. Almost certainly he could not cover them in one night or even day. All we know is that, having reached Portanellan, where Gregor Black Knee was now living with his family whilst he rebuilt the burned-out Glengyle House, the prisoner was then ferried out to the small island called Eilean Dhu in the loch, where amidst the tall frowning mountains he was held under guard in a primitive stone-and-turf hut for days whilst his fate was considered.

We do not know the details of what happened during the next few days, for no-one has left a written record of them, as is not to be wondered at. We do know, however, that Graham of Killearn plumbed the depths of fear and despair, and exhaustion also, so that he did exactly as he was told, and even wrote a letter dictated by Rob, to the Duke of Montrose, thus:

May it please Your Grace —
I am obliged to give Your Grace the trouble of this, by Robert Roy's commands, being so unfortunate at present to be his prisoner. I refer the way and manner I was apprehended to the bearer, and shall only in short acquaint Your Grace with the demands, which are, that Your Grace shall discharge him of all soumes he owes your Grace, and shall give him the soume of 3,400 merks for his loss and damages sustained by him, both at Craigroston and at his house, Auchinchisallen; and that Your Grace shall give your word not to trouble or prosecute him afterwards; till which time he carries me, all the money I received this day, my books and bonds for entress, not yet paid, along with him, with assurances of hard usage if any party

are sent after him. The soume I received this day, con-
firm to the nearest computation I can make before sev-
eral of the gentlemen, is £3,227-2-8 Scots, of which I
gave them notes. I shall wait Your Grace's return,
and ever am,

Your Grace's most obedient, faithful, humble
JOHN GRAHAME.

From such sources as we can glean information, we can only say for certain that the man's fate
remained undecided for some time. For once, Rob
Roy MacGregor was uncertain of himself. For
years he had waited for this day. He had sworn to
make Killearn pay with his life for what he had
done to Mary MacGregor. Rob must have brooded
endlessly on how he would exact his revenge. But
when it came to the bit, it was not so easy. It was
one thing to plan the daring coup at Chapellaroch,
and the kidnapping, at last, of the hated enemy;
altogether another to wreak the desired vengeance
on a helpless prisoner. Undoubtedly Rob would
have fought the matter out in a duel had Killearn
been a swordsman or a pistol shot. But he was neither — merely a somewhat flabby, middle-aged
man in extreme discomfort and misery. Whatever
else he was, Rob Roy had always been of a roman-
tic and heroic temperament. Faced with this distressing unheroic captive, he was nonplussed
indeed as to what to do.

Probably in his dilemma Rob turned to Mary
— almost inevitably so, for she was staying at the
time with Gregor and his wife at Portanellan, only
a mile away. Scott has painted her as a hard and
violent woman, soured by her sufferings. I feel
myself that, on the contrary, she most likely was
pressing Rob towards mercy to the man who had
injured her, convincing her fiery and dramatic hus-

band that charity and compassion was the better course, and that harsh vengeance now could by no means wipe the slate clean of what had been done that other November night, four years earlier. There is good reason to believe that Rob's relations with his wife which had been somewhat difficult and strained ever since that terrible event, hereafter took a sudden turn for the better, and they seem to have lived together happily from then on. If this is so, it surely must have been largely because his action towards Graham of Killearn pleased and comforted her.

At any rate, the bare facts of the matter are there before us. Rob Roy, after long swearing dire vengeance on his enemy, captured him on Monday, November 19th, 1716, held him prisoner in various places, but mainly on the island in Loch Katrine until the following Sunday, and then released him, unharmed, and with his ledgers, papers and so on — but not the Duke's money — a free man again. What transpired between the two men during those five days we do not know — but probably to be dismissed contemptuously at the end of them, unhurt, was in fact the greatest blow to Killearn's pride and self-esteem that could have been devised.

It may all seem something of an anti-climax to the reader — and no doubt it did to Rob himself, at the time. Nevertheless, we now can see that any other action would have been a great deal less to the credit of this strange man.

CHAPTER 14

Foul Play

MONTROSE, furious at his monetary loss as well as what had been done to his factor, redoubled his efforts against Rob Roy. He also saw in this an opportunity to attack his rival, the Duke of Argyll — for although Montrose was in charge of the government of Scotland, Argyll still had enormous influence and power in the land. Scotland, indeed, so recently split for or against the Union, for or against the Stewarts, was now splitting for or against Argyll and Montrose. The Secretary of State, who, as the Lord Justice Clerk wrote, was frightened to travel from his home area to Edinburgh by the direct Stirling route on account of Rob Roy's kidnapping ways, now ordered the new commander-in-chief not only to put a strong English garrison into Inversnaid and take the fullest military measures against the outlaw, but also told the Independent Companies of Militia to do the same. This was a shrewd move against Argyll — for the only Independent Companies in the area in which Rob Roy operated were Campbell ones, officered by Argyll's own lairds.

So there developed the farcical situation of the Campbell militia busily scouring the snow-bound hills for Rob Roy for two hard winter months — and not finding him — while all along Rob was dwelling, by the Duke's permission, in the Campbell glen of Shira only a mile or two from the Duke's castle!

In hot anger at this, Montrose took the drastic course of altogether disbanding the Independent Companies as unreliable — all of them, since he dared not single out the Duke's ones for such treatment.

Nothing could have suited Rob Roy better, of course. Although these militia companies had never done him much harm, they were always a force to be kept in mind as they acted in a manner similar to his own old Highland Watch in many ways. Now there were only regular soldiers charged with keeping the peace in Scotland — and not only was there not enough of them, but being mainly English or foreign mercenaries, they were not very good at soldiering in Highland territory. Rob had a freer hand in consequence. So had all other Highlanders interested in cattle-lifting. Obviously it was time that Rob started the Highland Watch again, officially or unofficially.

For the next year or so, two threads are most prominent in the tapestry of Rob Roy's dramatic life. Both stemmed from the feud between the two Dukes, Montrose and Argyll. On the one hand, just as Rob had foreseen, civil lawlessness increased in the Highlands, due to the suppressing of the Independent Companies and the presence of the many masterless men left by the Jacobite rising — for it must be remembered that there were no police forces in operation in those days. On the other hand, intrigues were going on all the time, on the part of Montrose and the faction in power, to bring down Argyll to the very dust. Strangely enough, these efforts very much involved Rob personally.

As to the lawlessness, this really became serious, with the swift and alarming rise in the theft of cattle, almost immediately the militia ceased to function. There can be no doubt at all that Rob himself was at the back of much of this; but equally surely there were plenty of others to take a hand, with nobody but the unfortunate farmers and cattle-owners themselves to take measures against the menace. All along the Highland Line, and far south also, the groan began to go up: 'Oh, for the Glengyle Watch, again! '

Privately, Rob began to visit clients.

Much more secret was the other thread of the tapestry — but this time the initiative lay with Rob's enemies. Montrose hated and feared Rob undoubtedly, but as became a Duke, he hated and feared the other Duke more. And Rob could be used to pull down Argyll.

The politics of the 18th century are murky indeed, and the case of the Duke of Argyll is a notable example. As we know, he had been accused of being too kind to the Jacobites, of bungling Sheriffmuir, and of failing to stamp out the embers of the Rising vigorously enough immediately afterwards, before he was dismissed. Now a new accusation crept in. It was suggested that all along he had been a secret Jacobite himself, deliberately betraying King George. And the man to prove this was Rob Roy.

Whether there was any basis of truth in this charge we cannot be sure. It certainly is possible. Rob's letter to Wade years afterwards, if genuine, admits that he did communicate with Argyll during the period prior to Sheriffmuir. The important matter here is that Rob did not admit it at this stage, when it would have been so much to his advantage to do so. He kept his mouth resolutely shut.

It was not Montrose himself, of course, who approached Rob the first time — though the proposals seem to have first come through his factor, Graham of Killearn. A meeting was arranged, a most secret meeting, at Cramond Bridge near Edinburgh, between Rob and the Lord Justice Clerk, Cockburn of Ormiston. This Ormiston was really the second man in Scotland at the time, but he was acting for Montrose. He offered Rob full pardon for all his activities, reversal of the outlawry sentence, restoration of his estates, and other benefits, if he would come forward publicly to testify against Argyll, to the effect that he and the Duke had indeed been in secret correspondence in the Jacobite favour while the latter was government commander-in-chief in Scotland. Rob refused blankly to betray the man who was now giving him shelter.

The next attempt came a few months later. By that time, Rob's plans for the revival of the Watch were far advanced — in fact, it was probably in operation again in a small way. But Glen Shira in Argyll was far too far away from the edge of the prosperous Lowlands to make a suitable base for the large-scale droving of cattle, and most of Rob's old stamping-grounds were either in Montrose's hands or under military surveillance. His eyes kept turning to his early haunts in Balquhidder, Atholl's property, not Montrose's and most convenient for his purposes. The large farm of Inverlochlarig Beg, away up at the head of the glen, miles above Monachyle Tuarach, and very safe from surprise attack, was vacant. Rob put feelers out to the Duke of Atholl. The farm could not be rented to an outlaw — but a friend's name would serve. And, of course, Atholl's great cattle interests would benefit also.

After some cautious preliminaries, it was agreed that Rob should call at Dunkeld House and see the Duke — secretly, needless to say, and under safe-conduct. But when the two met, for the first time for so many years, it turned out that it was not about the farm of Inverlochlarig that Atholl was concerned, but a very different matter — the old business of bringing down Argyll. Atholl had been got at, no doubt as the price of himself being received back into government favour, to assist in this matter. Once again all the benefits which would accrue to Rob were brought forward — this time adding official acceptance of the restored Watch, and of course, Inverlochlarig Beg.

When Rob once again indignantly refused to betray Argyll, Atholl showed his teeth. He had Rob arrested there and then, claiming that the safe-conduct had been signed by his brother, Lord Edward Murray, and did not bind himself. Rob was a prisoner once again.

If this was treacherous practice, it was typical of the times. The government much approved of Atholl's loyal action, at any rate, and King George himself sent a message that he was well pleased with His Grace's care and diligence on this occasion. The Lord Justice Clerk ordered Rob to be brought into Edinburgh and lodged in the Castle which he declared, 'is the best prison the King has'.

But Rob Roy MacGregor, as these lofty gentlemen should have known by this time, if not easy to catch, was still more difficult to hold. A strong military detachment was sent north to fetch him to

Edinburgh, but meantime he was held imprisoned at Logierait near Dunkeld, under armed guard.

Rob seems to have come well supplied with money on this occasion — possibly he had intended to clinch the Inverlochlarig deal by paying his rent in advance and he now spent it liberally in buying liquor for himself and his jailers. Probably the latter, being Highland Murrays, were somewhat ashamed of the way in which he had been trapped, and sympathised with a man going to Edinburgh Castle, possibly to his death. They humoured him in his drinking, at any rate, and did not refuse his generous hospitality. Soon Rob seemed very drunk, and his captors were merry. He insisted on more and more liquor being purchased, and when the guards were far from vigilant and he himself appeared to be quite helpless, he abruptly exploded into typical action, bursting out of the gaol, leaping on to one of the horses outside, and galloping off before his bewildered warders could do anything effective to stop him. Needless to say, he got clean away.

Atholl's new-found popularity with the Government dropped sharply. Angry and upset, he quickly put a new tenant into Inverlochlarig Beg, with a squadron of troopers quartered in Balquhidder to see that he was not put out again.

Rob bided his time but he had an answer to this, too. He would show Atholl what it meant to hoodwink and betray Rob Roy MacGregor. He wrote a pamphlet, in the form of a letter to all who loved honour and honesty, setting forth the infamy of those in power, of Montrose, Lord Justice Clerk Ormiston, and Atholl himself, in seeking to make him bear false witness against the Duke of Argyll, and saw that this pamphlet had wide distribution. It was, of course, an age of pamphleteering. But that was not all. He proceeded with the revived Watch activities, and left the new tenant of Inverlochlarig alone until the troopers were withdrawn from Balquhidder. Then he went to see the tenant secretly.

We can imagine the unfortunate man's state of mind at this interview. But Rob was gentle, reasonable, persuasive. He did not go in for any dramatics. Instead of seeking to throw the man out, he came to a working agreement with him. Since the lease could not be in Rob's outlawed name anyway, the present tenant's name was good enough. Let him stay on in Inverlochlarig Beg — but as Rob's nominee and lieutenant. He would not suffer for it, to be sure.

Undoubtedly the man found this solution much better than anything he had expected. He agreed — and soon upper Balquhidder was again a busy centre of Rob Roy's activities, and was to remain so.

Whether Atholl realised fully what had happened we do not know. But if so, he seems to have decided to shut his eyes to what he was unable to mend.

CHAPTER 15

Spanish Invasion

THE Highland Watch was once more functioning vigorously, successfully, with peace and security returning to the troubled lands where the Highlands and Lowlands meet. It is clear that, by and large, the lairds, landowners and farmers welcomed its return wholeheartedly, as much the lesser of two evils. It may not have been a semi-official body, as formerly, but the authorities seem to have made little attempt to suppress it — apart from Montrose's own private vendetta against Rob, its leader. The following years are full of stories concerning Rob's activities on this score, and his methods of convincing reluctant or backsliding clients that their course was a foolish one. He seems to have succeeded almost entirely in this — at least, we hear of none of the protests and independent actions of the objectors being successful. The Watch went from strength to strength. All cattle-lifting, by others, was sternly put down, and the cattle trade was thriving again.

So a couple of years passed. Then, quite suddenly, as a result of some murky political manoeuvre, Argyll was back in favour in London. I have never discovered the reasons behind this. Clearly Montrose was just as bitterly against him as ever, and was still accusing him of Jacobite sympathies and perhaps with some reason, for we read that next year, when King George seems to have reached a new level of unpopularity, King James in France began to believe that he might soon find himself being called to the throne, and expected the Duke of Argyll to be foremost in assisting him in this course. Be that as it may, in 1719 the Duke was restored to his offices and created Baron Chatham and Earl and Duke of Greenwich in the peerage of Great Britain, re-admitted to the Privy Council, and given the appointment of Lord Great Chamberlain. This undoubtedly aided Rob Roy further in his climb back to prosperity, for he could not but gain by the increased power of his protector.

That Montrose was all too well aware of this is illustrated by an amusing clash between the two Dukes over Rob Roy — not on their native heath but within the august portals of the Privy Council itself, in London. Apparently Montrose, stung to renewed anger by an attack by Rob, in the January of that year, on one of the principal Montrose tenants, Graham of Drunkie, and the theft of a large number of his beasts, declared before the Council that this most notorious rebel and outlaw was being harboured by a certain nobleman who ought to know better. Argyll did not fail to take him up.

'I am well acquainted with the man,' he said, 'and it is true that I have allowed him wood and water on my land, as I do the meanest of my clan. But I would be sorry to think that there was any harm in this; for it is common knowledge that Your Grace has been yet more generous, keeping Rob Roy in beef and grain for many years past!'

No doubt the English Privy Councillors were much mystified.

Montrose could not do much about Argyll now, but he could still try to bring Rob to book. Receiving word that Rob was using a certain house in Glen Falloch, at the head of Loch Lomond, he sent a party of regular soldiers on a swift and secret mission to waylay him there. But Rob had his own informers, and escaped from the house in time, returning after dark with 50 armed Gregorach to surprise the house, in which the military were now spending the night. Their approach seems to have been spotted by a sentry, who fired, and a general exchange of shots, followed, in which one soldier was killed. Rob drew off his men until morning, when the military set off for the south again. Whereupon he ambushed the troop in his usual expert manner. This time he appeared to have contented himself with disarming them all, and sending them unharmed on their way, with messages for Montrose — perhaps the Watch was running short of arms and ammunition.

That this open attack on regular troops was not followed up by severe reprisals — or any action by the new Lord Great Chamberlain — shows how powerful was Argyll's championship of the outlaw, and of course how scanty was the respect, even in the highest quarters, for law and order at that period.

But no doubt the authorities had greater worries on their minds. That same spring, in April 1719, still another Jacobite Rising was attempted in Highland Scotland. This one seems to have been a curiously sudden and unpremeditated affair, rather mysterious indeed, a rising nobody appears to know a great deal about. First, three ships arrived quite unexpectedly in the sea loch of Loch Alsh, between the mainland and Skye, bringing about 300 Spanish soldiers and four of the exiled leaders of the Rising of 1715, including Atholl's heir, the Marquis of Tullibardine, and the chief of the Mackenzies, the Earl of Seaforth. Here they took over Eilean Donan Castle, a MacKenzie stronghold traditionally held for the chiefs by the MacRaes, and sent the bulk of their force further up Loch Duich to hold the pass of Glen Shiel, almost the only land link with the rest of Scotland. From Eilean Donan the fiery cross was once again sent out to the clans.

Not unnaturally perhaps the clans were less than enthusiastic in their welcome. Other notables arrived from France, including Tullibardine's brother, Lord George Murray, Cameron of Locheil, and Brigadier Mackintosh of Borlum. But even with all these leaders back in the country, the Jacobites were unwilling to rise for a third attempt. A much greater Spanish force was alleged to be on the way, under the Duke of Ormond — Spain was at present at war with England over the American colonies, and undoubtedly, from their point of view, this was just a Spanish diversion in that struggle. The chiefs in Scotland, going by past experience, were on the whole inclined to wait until they saw the Stewarts' foreign allies actually in the flesh before they again committed themselves.

Not so Rob Roy MacGregor, however. Despite the fact that he had now struggled back to a fair level of security and prosperity, and was risking all once more, he threw himself into this new attempt with his usual enthusiasm for the cause, in spite of Gregor of Glengyle's refusal to partake on this occasion. Those who insist on casting doubt on

Rob's genuineness in Jacobite support should recognise this. He marched north without the Glengyle contingent, with only 40 men of his own, and joined Tullibardine in Glen Shiel. Very few other clans had in fact sent contingents as yet. There were a good number of local MacKenzies and MacRaes assembled, some Camerons, MacDonalds, MacKinnons and others, totalling only about 1200 men.

Still the large Spanish invasion force did not turn up; it had actually been scattered and dispersed before by a great storm off Cape Finisterre. Some English warships did arrive, however, and under the threat of the cannon, Eilean Donan had to be given up. The small army in Glen Shiel waited, in some doubt as to what to do next.

The Government had been waiting too. General Wightman, at Inverness, was the present commander in the Highlands, but he had no large number of troops to face a new revolt.

When it became obvious, however, that the clans did not appear to be rising this time, or at least, not yet — Wightman set off for the west with about 2000 men, including four battalions of regular infantry, a mixed force of cavalry, and a contingent of Whig clans from the North-east, Munroes, Rosses and Sutherlands.

The Battle of Glen Shiel, fought on June 11th, 1719, was indeed no true battle. There seems to have been a great lack of liaison between the Spaniards and the Highlanders who held the steep pass. Wightman's troops do not appear to have distinguished themselves either. He had brought along many mortars with which he bombarded the Jacobite positions, but they do not seem to have done a lot of damage. It was very bad country for cavalry, of course — a very steep and wind-

PART OF THE NORTH-WEST HIGHLAND COASTLINE
SHOWING THE AREA OF THE BATTLE OF GLEN SHIEL

ing rocky glen. A certain amount of skirmishing went on, with long-range musket fire, but no close fighting. The Jacobites held a very strong position, and waited therein — a procedure which would never commend itself to the impetuous Highland sword-fighters, however much the Spaniards may have approved of it. Night fell with Wightman still not having made any major attack.

Unfortunately, though the Jacobites were said to have lost only one man killed against the government's 20, amongst those wounded was the Earl of Seaforth. chief of the MacKenzies, whose clan made up the largest body of troops present. Disgruntled by this, and by the fact that they had been kept inactive all day in the face of mortar and musket fire, they seem to have dispersed to their homes during the night. One contingent from a small clan also marched off, declaring that they had only come for one day's fighting as an obligation to their friend Seaforth! In the morning, amongst the swirling mountain mists, the Spaniards, from their high position on the hillside, decided that they had been deserted by the Highlanders, and marched out to surrender to Wightman — who must have been very surprised to receive them. That pointed mountain is still called Sgurr na Spainteach, the Peak of the Spaniards, to this day. Thereafter, the main body of the Highlanders melted away.

Nobody gained much credit from Glen Shiel. But Rob Roy at least, with his Gregorach, did something useful. In the retreat, he alone appears to have thought of the stores of arms and ammunition cached at Kintail. Rather than let this fall into government hands, he and his men went out of their way to blow it up, before heading discreetly southwards into the wild mountains.

That was the end of the so-called Rising of 1719.

CHAPTER 16

'I Return No More'

ROB ROY escaped any direct reprisals for his part in this inglorious affair. Probably, indeed, there was no proof that he had been present. Anyway, if the authorities could not lay hands on him over his outlawry and cattle-lifting, there was no reason to believe that they could do better on a charge of treason. He seems to have returned quietly to business as usual and the work of the Watch, while the Government had to look the other way.

The years that followed were not eventful ones, as far as written history is concerned — for Rob himself or for the generality of folk in Scotland. From 1720 until the outbreak of the great Jacobite Rising of 1745, led by Bonnie Prince Charlie, King James's son, comparative peace settled on a troubled Scotland. Undoubtedly the country was sick and tired of civil war. Nevertheless, legends and traditions continue to tell a colourful story of Rob Roy's exploits for many a year yet — the same kind of dashing adventures and shrewd manoeuvres as before, only without political significance. However, Rob was not so young as he once had been, and it is probable that he did indeed begin to take life a little more easily. He was now a man of over 50 — and, though still vigorous and active, must frequently have longed for a more settled life. More and more, it is clear, Gregor of Glengyle was taking over the day-to-day direction of the Watch.

Rob was now firmly established at Inverlochlarig Beg in Balquhidder — presumably still in the name of the tenant put in by Atholl, for there is no word of him having made official peace with the Duke. It was an extraordinary situation — but then these were extraordinary times, to our eyes. If Atholl had no effective means of expelling Rob from his land, and was quite unable to bring him to what passed for justice in those days, then I suppose he was wise just to shut his eyes to Rob's activities on one of his farms especially as this more or less guaranteed the safety of the Atholl flocks and herds from the attentions of cattle-lifters. It became a case of live and let live. Besides, Atholl, like Rob himself, was not so young as he had been, and was a sick man. He died in 1724. His Jacobite sons, of course, were well-disposed towards Rob Roy, and unlikely to wish to dispossess him. At any rate, he remained at Inverlochlarig Beg in Balquhidder for the remainder of his life.

I said that Rob escaped any direct reprisals for his participation in the 1719 Jacobite affair at Glen Shiel. Indirect repercussions did, however, affect him, as they did all the Highlands. For, as an eventual result of this attempt, in 1724 the Government made a really serious and calculated effort to pacify and subdue the wild Highlands — and this time they were much more successful than hitherto. Wisely, although they did it by means of soldiers, this was not so much a military campaign as an engineering one. They decided, and rightly, that so long as the Highlands remained a roadless and trackless wilderness, the Government would be unable to exert any real authority over them and the clans which inhabited them. So they appointed Major-General Wade as commander-in-chief in Scotland, and sent him north into the Highlands to build roads and bridges.

Wade was a remarkable man. He may well have been an excellent soldier and tactician since he was promoted to field-marshal in due course. His enduring fame, however, rests not on his soldiering but on his road-making. For years he laboured patiently, firmly, vigorously, despite all the set-backs of a most difficult terrain, a harsh climate and a hostile population, to drive his roads through that area, more than half of all Scotland, where hitherto the only kind of roads known were deer tracks, pony tracks and drove roads — these last, of course, mere routes over which herds of cattle might be driven, not actual roadways. As everyone who knows the Highlands even a little is well aware, it is a land of high mountains, steep rocky glens, peat moss, great lochs and innumerable rushing torrents. Roads meant bridges — bridges by the hundred, the thousand — cuttings, embankments, ferries; endless surveying, quarrying, designing, and endless labour.

For years Wade and his engineers worked away, even though floods washed away their efforts, Highlanders destroyed the bridges and attacked his roadmen, bogs swallowed up his materials, rain and snow reduced his labour force. It is to the credit of the Government that, weak and feeble as it was, it did support Wade for so long in this seemingly hopeless and endless task, year after year. One could write a long and exciting book about General Wade and his Highland road-building. Here, all that can be said is that eventually he was successful. And for the first time in history, the Scottish Highlands were largely opened up to travellers from outside.

At first, of course, it was almost wholly soldiers who travelled over these new and dangerous roads. No longer were the clans secure in their mountains. Military posts and forts were set up at intervals along the main routes, to defend them and keep the areas in submission — and though the roads and especially the bridges were constantly attacked and damaged by the clansmen, they were repaired, and severe examples made of those caught or suspected of sabotage. Wade could be harsh as well as patient and industrious. Gradually, the Redcoats, as the government troops were called, began to penetrate all but the most remote glens and straths of the far North-west. The days of fairly complete Highland immunity to southern law and order were nearly over.

It did not take years for the chiefs of the Central Highland clans to see all this, whatever those in the secure North-west and the islands might say. The government did not want trouble, and made it clear that written submissions to General Wade, and promises of future good conduct, would be accepted from all chiefs, even those deeply concerned in the late risings, with no reprisals or further persecutions. The chiefs were not so foolish as to refuse. A letter of submission, especially in the despised foreign English language, meant no more than the paper on which it was written — not like a good Gaelic oath sworn on a sword hilt, for instance. Almost with one accord the chiefs began to write their letters to the commander-in-chief, all in the most florid and fulsome style of the times, as though all dictated by the same servile pen. They did not mean a lot, for most of the writers or their sons were out again in Prince Charlie's rising 20 years later. Nevertheless, they represented the end of a chapter in Highland history.

It is here that we must deal with Rob Roy's own much criticised letter of submission to Wade, undated but apparently written some time in 1725. Scott quotes it in the appendix to his *Rob Roy*, saying that it was addressed to Field-Marshal Wade which of course is an error, for he was not made a field-marshal until many years later. He adds in a footnote: 'This curious epistle is copied from an authentic narrative of Marshal Wade's proceedings in the Highlands, communicated by the late eminent antiquary, George Chalmers Esq., to Mr Robert Jamieson of the Register House, Edinburgh and published in the Appendix to an Edition of Burt's *Letters From the North of Scotland.*'

There seems to be at least the possibility that this letter is not genuine. It was an age of forgery and written deceit. But assuming that it is genuine, even so I do not think that we ought to take it literally or to put upon it the interpretation that Scott has done, and as so many have automatically followed him in doing — namely that Rob Roy was either betraying, or preparing to betray the Jacobite cause at the time of Sheriffmuir. I think it is only fair to quote the entire letter, long as it is — for if I have herein portrayed Rob Roy MacGregor as very much a man in the heroic mould it is honest to add this very unheroic letter also. Here it is :

Sir — The great humanity with which you have constantly acted in the discharge of the trust reposed in you, and your ever having made use of the great powers with which you were vested, as the means of doing good and charitable offices to such as ye found proper objects of compassion, will, I hope, excuse my importunity in endeavouring to approve myself not absolutely unworthy of that mercy and favour which your Excellency has so generously procured from his Majesty for others in my unfortunate circumstances. I am very sensible nothing can be alleged sufficient to excuse so great a crime as I have been guilty of, that of Rebellion. But I humbly beg leave to lay before your Excellency some particulars in the circumstance of my guilt, which, I hope, will extenuate it in some measure. It was my misfortune, at the time the Rebellion broke out, to be liable to legal diligence and caption, at the Duke of Montrose's instance, for debt alleged due to him. To avoid being flung into prison, as I must certainly have been, had I followed my real inclinations in joining the King's troops at Stirling I was forced to take party with the adherents of the Pretender; for the country being all in arms, it was neither safe nor indeed possible for me to stand neuter. I should not, however, plead my being forced into that unnatural Rebellion against his Majesty King George, if I could not at the same time assure your Excellency, that I not only avoided acting offensively against his Majesty's forces upon all occasions, but on the contrary, sent his Grace the Duke of Argyll all the intelligence I could from time to time of the strength and situation of the Rebels; which I hope his Grace will do me the justice to acknowledge. As to the debt to the Duke of Montrose, I have discharged it to the utmost farthing. I beg your Excellency would be persuaded that, had it been in my power, as it was in my inclination, I should always have acted for the service of his Majesty King George, and that one reason of my begging the favour of your intercession

> *with his Majesty for the pardon of my life, is the*
> *earnest desire I have to employ it in his service,*
> *whose goodness, justice, and humanity, are so con-*
> *spicuous to all mankind.*
>
> > *I am, with all duty and respect,*
> > *Your Excellency's most &c,*
> > ROBERT CAMPBELL

As to comment on this extraordinary and unpleasing effusion from the man who had been one of the most active and vigorous Jacobites all his life, and an enemy of King George's government from its inception, responsible for acting offensively against his Majesty's forces at every opportunity right up to the time of writing and long after, all that can be said is that the letter is so untruthful, so ridiculously so, as to make it almost pointless to argue over the details of parts which may conceivably be true. I shall not attempt to do so, being quite content that Rob's whole life, and attitude to life, give the lie to what is written here, even if he wrote it himself.

The part which sticks in so many throats, of course, is where he declares that he sent to Argyll all the intelligence he could of the strength and situation of the rebels. This, at first glance, does seem like a damning admission of treachery. But is it so? Is it not much more likely, and in accord with Rob's amply revealed character and his long-standing loyalties, that he was here admitting, for political purposes, what he knew that the Government already knew — that he had indeed been in touch with Argyll at that time, but that this had not been in the government interest but in the Jacobite? In other words, that the treachery was not on Rob's part but on the Duke's. His addition to this sentence, 'which I hope his Grace will do me the justice to acknowledge', is, I think, significant. If all along Rob was in touch with Argyll, as the Government itself alleged, helping to keep him at least half a Jacobite, and enabling him as commander-in-chief to be gentle towards the Jacobite cause, then Rob should have earned the thanks of all Jacobites, not their condemnation. The fact that Mar and the other leaders, including King James himself, continued to trust him and use his services thereafter at every opportunity, seems to substantiate this. That Rob used these circumstances to commend himself to the Government 10 years afterwards, in this spate of formal submissions to Wade, may seem to us neither ethical nor suitable — but nevertheless, the quirk of it, the cunning turning of the tables, could be very typically Rob Roy. No harm would be done to any, and he might turn the situation to his own advantage.

I have gone into this vexed matter at great length, for this letter, if genuine, is vastly important in any assessment of Rob Roy's complicated character. None of us is all white or all black, wholly good or wholly bad; this is especially so of men of tremendous enthusiasm and energy, and in times of perpetual civil strife, oppression, weak government and lawlessness. I think that I may leave the reader to make his own judgment: whether in fact Rob Roy was a hero or a scoundrel — or something of both.

Whether this letter served Rob any useful purpose is not known. It may have helped in the reversal of the old sentence of outlawry — although it is uncertain if this was ever officially reversed, however little it appears to have troubled Rob Roy hereafter.

The last 10 years of Rob's life are not well documented or written up. But undoubtedly he did not merely fade away, as old soldiers are said to do. Local traditions are very clear on that. He went on to the end, more or less as he had always done, if less vigorously. He seems to have come to a kind of truce with the Duke of Montrose. The Duke, of course, was more and more in London, and Rob's activities doubtless infuriated him the less; and for Rob's part, the Watch, under Gregor's strong hands, was growing ever more respectable and profitable, so that the urge to bait Montrose would be largely gone. Moreover, Rob was no longer driven to humiliate and score off Killearn.

Nevertheless, there are innumerable legends detailing Rob's continuing adventures during this period of his life. Many of them, no doubt, are pure or part fiction, but there are enough to indicate that the old fiery spirit still burned brightly. After recounting so many, it would be a weariness to relate more of them here. Two last death-bed stories must suffice, to prove that Rob Roy was himself to the end.

One is significant in that it implies that, although all along an upholder of the Kirk of Scotland, in the Presbyterian faith, he was at heart a Catholic. For, at the age of 64, he fell seriously ill and decided that his last hours had come, he got Mary to send for a priest, but not the parish minister, rather one Father Drummond, chaplain of the Jacobite Earl of Perth at Drummond Castle. The story goes that the priest, when he realised that Rob was indeed mortally ill, said that the sick man must make his confession. Rob seems to have been slightly reluctant to do this — as well he might — but the priest gently insisted. So the old freebooter confessed carefully to sundry small sins that were hardly of the sort that could be held seriously against him if he got better, and the priest appeared to be satisfied. Except for one point; he asserted that before he could shrive him, Rob must declare that he forgave all his enemies. This seemed to Rob to be carrying things altogether too far, and he began to argue. But his strength was failing, and he could not battle against Father Drummond's determination, insistent on Rob's salvation. At length he mumbled that he forgave various individuals, whom he named, for all that they had done against him. The priest listened — and when Rob had obviously finished, mentioned that he had not heard the name of a certain John MacLaren. Rob had recently quarrelled violently with this man over the tenancy of the farm of Invernenty, which he wanted for one of his MacGregors and which MacLaren had managed to gain. There was probably more to it than this, from what transpired later — but at any rate MacLaren had been left out of Rob's forgiveness. The priest was adamant, however; no benediction until MacLaren was forgiven. Rob it is claimed, then raised his eyes to the foot of the bed, where his younger son Robin Og stood watching.

'I forgive my enemies, especially John Mac-Laren,' he panted. To add, catching Robin's eye. 'But see *you* to him!'

He got his blessing.

It is thought to have been the same John MacLaren who featured in the second story, which presumably happened almost immediately afterwards. A large number of Rob's friends and neighbours, hearing of his sudden and serious illness, came hurrying to his bedside to see him and pay their respects. After the long queue of them had filed past, and the dying man lay back exhausted, it was revealed to him that one more man waited outside to see him — John MacLaren. With a last spurt of energy, Rob's eyes lit up with something of their old fire. He would not have any MacLaren gloating over his weakness and downfall.

'Raise me in this bed,' he commanded Mary. 'Put my plaid around me. Bring my sword, my dirk and my pistol. It shall never be said that an enemy saw Rob Roy MacGregor defenceless and unarmed.'

So when the visitor was led in, it was to find the dying man looking as fierce as ever, indeed almost ready to do battle there and then with any interloping and upstart MacLaren. Much put out, the latter blurted out a few condolences, indicating that he had been misled about the state of Rob's health, while the sick man maintained a cold and haughty politeness. As the astonished visitor was led away, Rob succumbed.

He whispered to Mary. 'The piper ... bring him in ... to play *I Return No More.*' This was the traditional parting tune.

Rob is reputed to have died before the dirge was finished.

These stories may not be entirely factual — although it would be a brave man who attempted to deny them in the Rob Roy country. They have been handed down over the generations as a very vital tradition; at least they are in keeping with the known character of the man and it would not be in the least surprising if they were quite true. What is surprising, of course, is that Rob Roy MacGregor should have died in his bed, at all. Few men can have led a life of more continual risk, danger and excitement. It seems improbable, to say the least of it, that he should have lived to be the then ripe old age of 64, and ended up in his own house at Inverlochlarig Beg, between the sheets.

He died on the last day of 1734, and was buried

in the little churchyard of the Kirk of Balquhidder, where his grave is pointed out to this day.

Rob Roy MacGregor was a strange man, quite a little larger than life, living in a strange period in Scotland's history. His virtues probably have been exaggerated, as undoubtedly his faults have been. But whatever else he was, he was a MAN, dynamic, vehement, positive as well as picturesque. He has stamped his name indelibly on the colourful history of Scotland — which is quite a feat in itself, in a land which has produced so many outstanding and dramatic characters, a race of individualists. All over the world the name of Rob Roy is known, when practically all the others of his day and generation are forgotten. That is perhaps as good an epitaph as any.

It is perhaps relevant to add that just 10 years after Rob Roy's death there at last broke out the great Jacobite Rising of 1745, so much more impressive an affair than its predecessors, when Prince Charles Edward, with better leadership and greater forces, so nearly gained the throne for his melancholy father, marching victoriously from the Highlands as far south as Derby, with King George all packed and ready to flee London — but at Derby to turn back, much against his own wishes, on the advice of his generals. That Rising ended in the disaster of Culloden a year later and the subsequent savageries of the victorious Duke of Cumberland which forever earned him the title of 'Butcher'. That was to be the last of militant Jacobitism.

Yet still today in Scotland, the people have an affection for that lost and squandered cause. Moreover, even yet, the worth and advantages of the Union with England are a constant matter for debate; a great many Scots urging not so much its cancellation but its amendment, for the evils and neglects of long-range government are as real today as in the 18th century, and in many respects Scotland feels herself to suffer from a lack of understanding and interest on the part of London government, an inability to make the most of her own resources of men, skills and materials, and the lack of self-respect of an ancient, proud people who are not allowed to manage their own affairs. A majority now feel that Scotland would make a better partner in the United Kingdom if she once again had her own legislature in Edinburgh. Perhaps our memories are too long?

Bonnie Prince Charlie's campaign still raises the tempers and voices in Scotland, and the date 1745 sounds an ominous note in every Scots ear. In that last campaign, Colonel Gregor MacGregor of Glengyle led the Glengyle Regiment throughout with bravery and success. In fact he was one of the few Jacobite leaders that survived to come out of it all with a quite untarnished reputation.

The same cannot be said of Rob's eldest son, Major James Mor MacGregor, who despite some brilliant and gallant military feats stained his name at the end by turning against his former comrades-in-arms. As for Robin Og, he led a wild and undisciplined life, unredeemed by the chivalry and glamour of his father's character. He shot John MacLaren dead whilst the man was ploughing at Invernenty a few months after Rob's death. For this, he seems to have escaped justice but, after serving as a soldier, he was eventually apprehended for other disgraceful activities, tried and executed in 1754. The rest of Rob's family do not seem to have distinguished themselves. In fact, his sons were little credit to him. Perhaps their father was partly to blame for this — for he always seems to have preferred his nephew, Gregor Black Knee, to any of them; and their upbringing must have been a very difficult one.

But then, who can name the heroes' sons who turn out to be heroes, in the long tale of history?

BIBLIOGRAPHY

Rob Roy. Sir Walter Scott (Nelson Classics).

Highland Constable. Hamilton Howlett (Blackwood), 1950.

History of Rob Roy. A. H. Millar, 1883.

Memoirs of Rob Roy. Kenneth Macleay, 1881.

History of the Clan Gregor. Murray MacGregor (Wm. Brown), 1898-1901.

History of the Scottish Highlands, Clans and Regiments. John S. Keltie, 1875.

Historic Haunts of Scotland. Alex. Maclehose (Maclehose), 1936.

In the Hills of Breadalbane. V. A. Firsoff (Hale), 1954.

R. L. Stevenson and the Scottish Highlands. D. B. Morris (Mackay), 1929.

INDEX